*FAST*READS

SUMMARY BUNDLE

FIND YOUR FOCUS

Includes Summary of Essentialism,
Summary of The Checklist Manifesto,
Summary of Designing Your Life,
Summary of The One Thing,
and Summary of The Obstacle Is the Way

TABLES OF CONTENTS

SUMMARY of ESSENTIALISM 5

EXECUTIVE SUMMARY 6
PART I: ESSENCE 9
PART II: EXPLORE 13
PART III: ELIMINATE 19
PART IV: EXECUTE 28
APPENDIX: Leadership Essentials 36

SUMMARY of THE CHECKLIST MANIFESTO ... 37

EXECUTIVE SUMMARY 38
INTRODUCTION...39
CHAPTER 1: THE PROBLEM OF EXTREME COMPLEXITY 41
CHAPTER 2: THE CHECKLIST 42
CHAPTER 3: THE END OF THE MASTER BUILDER 44
CHAPTER 4: THE IDEA 46
CHAPTER 5: THE FIRST TRY 48
CHAPTER 6: THE CHECKLIST FACTORY 50
CHAPTER 7: THE TEST 52
CHAPTER 8: THE HERO IN THE AGE OF CHECKLISTS 54
CHAPTER 9: THE SAVE 56

SUMMARY of DESIGNING YOUR LIFE 57

EXECUTIVE SUMMARY 58
INTRODUCTION: LIFE BY DESIGN 59
CHAPTER 1: START WHERE YOU ARE 62
CHAPTER 2: BUILDING A COMPASS 65
CHAPTER 3: WAYFINDING...67
CHAPTER 4: GETTING UNSTUCK 70
CHAPTER 5: DESIGN YOUR LIVES 72
CHAPTER 6: PROTOTYPING..74
CHAPTER 7: HOW NOT TO GET A JOB....................................76
CHAPTER 8: DESIGNING YOUR DREAM JOB 78
CHAPTER 9: CHOOSING HAPPINESS......................................80

CHAPTER 10: FAILURE IMMUNITY 82

CHAPTER 11: BUILDING A TEAM 84

CONCLUSION: A WELL-DESIGNED LIFE 86

SUMMARY of THE ONE THING............................ 87

EXECUTIVE SUMMARY...88

PART 1: THE LIES They Mislead and Derail Us 92

PART II: THE TRUTH The Simple Path to Productivity 98

PART III: EXTRAORDINARY RESULTS Unlocking the Possibilities Within You..101

EDITORIAL REVIEW 109

SUMMARY of THE OBSTACLE IS THE WAY.... 110

EXECUTIVE SUMMARY 111

INTRODUCTION...112

PART I: PERCEPTION 113

PART II – ACTION 119

PART III – WILL..126

SUMMARY
of
ESSENTIALISM

The Disciplined Pursuit of Less

by Greg McKeown

*A FastReads Book Summary with
Key Takeaways & Analysis*

EXECUTIVE SUMMARY

In this book, Greg McKeown explores the systematic discipline of essentialism and reveals how anyone can discover what is absolutely essential and live a more purposeful and productive life. In his view, the essentialist lives and works by design: he explores the activities that contribute to his most important purpose, actively eliminates everything else, and creates a routine that makes the execution of the essential effortless.

McKeown draws on personal experience and years of practice as a business coach to show how anyone can realize his highest point of contribution by harnessing the power of choice and investing in only a few important activities. He contends that by focusing on "less but better", individuals, teams, and organizations can make a million miles of progress in one direction rather than a millimeter of progress in a million directions.

CHAPTER 1: The Essentialist

Sam Elliot, an executive in Silicon Valley, was struggling to keep up with the requests of his superiors when a mentor advised him to only take up tasks that he deemed essential. If he analyzed a request and found that he did not have the resources to complete it on time – or if he found that the request was not the most important use of his time – he politely declined. While the people he said "no" to were disappointed at first, they came to respect him for his honesty. By evaluating requests with these criteria, Elliot was able to make progress towards the things that really mattered and get back time for his family.

The essentialist gives himself permission to stop trying to do everything. In so doing, he focuses on what is vital and, subsequently, makes meaningful contributions in core areas of his work and life. The essentialist knows he is constantly surrounded by noise. His ultimate goal is to filter through the noise to find the few things that are essential. Essentialism is, by definition, the pursuit of less but better.

The essentialist channels his energy and resources to few activities so as to make significant progress in few but essential areas. He understands that making meaningful achievement in the areas that matter most requires real trade-offs. In contrast, the nonessentialist pursues several projects at once and only makes minute progress in each project.

Because the nonessentialist thinks everything is important, he says "yes" to most of the requests that come his way. He takes on more work simply to please. As he takes on more requests, the quality of his work suffers and he feels perpetually overwhelmed and exhausted. The essentialist stops to consider what really matters before taking on tasks. By analyzing tradeoffs and saying "no" to the nonessential, he takes control of his work and lives a satisfying life.

Paradoxically, the pursuit of success is often the catalyst for failure. The clarity of purpose that initially leads one to success diminishes as he seeks – or is presented – with more opportunities. With increasing opportunities, it is very easy to lose sight of one's highest point of contribution.

The pursuit of more has exploded over the last decade as a result of a number of interconnected trends. For one, increasing choices have overwhelmed people's ability to manage priorities. The pressure to make decisions that are socially acceptable and the widespread belief that one can have it all has further undermined focus on what's essential. When you lose sight of what's important, other people – your colleagues, boss, friends, and family – make their agendas your priority.

The essentialist **evaluates** activities based on the contribution they make towards his goal and **eliminates** those that do not make any meaningful contribution. He goes further and creates a system that removes the obstacles that keep piling up so that he can **execute** his intentions as effortlessly as possible.

Key Takeaways

• Essentialism is a conscious decision to eliminate the noise of the trivial many and invest in a few vital activities.

• The undisciplined pursuit of more is a leading cause of failure for iconic companies and the people who work in them.

• When many things are a priority, nothing is a priority.

PART I: ESSENCE

What is the Core Logic of an Essentialist?

Essentialism is a way of thinking, the goal of which is to do everything differently. The eternal challenge of the essentialist is to conquer the assumption that everything is important, that he *has* to do, and that he can do everything. He replaces these assumptions with the belief that only a few things are truly important, that he has a choice, and that he can do anything but not everything.

CHAPTER 2: CHOOSE: The Invincible Power of Choice

People or circumstances may take away the options you have, but they cannot take your ability to choose.

"The ability to choose cannot be taken away or even given away— it can only be forgotten."

People forget that they are always free to choose because the outcome of past circumstances has conditioned them to believe they are helpless. An employee who has failed to deliver on a project, for example, may check out when given a similar project because he believes his efforts won't matter. Alternatively, he may take on every assignment or challenge that comes his way because he believes he has no choice but to do it all.

Making choices tends to be difficult because saying "no" feels like a loss. Before anything else, an essentialist recognizes his ability to choose and understands that this ability exists separately from the options he has. The nonessentialist loses his right to choose when he believes he *has* to do something. He takes on a helpless attitude by forgetting he has a choice to choose and, subsequently, becomes a function of his past choices or other people's choices.

Key Takeaways

• Every time you sacrifice your power to choose, a circumstance or someone steps in and makes a decision you would not have consciously made.

• The essentialist recognizes there's always a choice. He understands that his ability to choose is separate from the options available.

CHAPTER 3: DISCERN: The Unimportance of Practically Everything

Working hard does not always produce better results, especially when you are working hard on the unimportant. Better results are almost always realized by working less but better on a few things that have a direct impact on your success metrics. Ferran Adria, for example, has become one of the world's greatest chefs by reducing dishes to their essence, serving only fifty people per night (and canceling most of the two million requests for dinner reservations he gets each year), and closing his restaurant for six months a year to refine his craft.

While doing more may seem like an obvious way to increase productivity, research shows that more efforts often forestall progress. Channeling efforts to a few vital elements instead – as advocated for by the Pareto Principle – produces significant improvement in quality and productivity. Everyday applications of the Pareto Principle are evident everywhere; Warren Buffet has become one of the most successful investors of all time by making big bets on a few sure investments and disregarding numerous investments that are merely good.

Key Takeaways

• At least 80-percent (or almost everything) of the requests you get or the tasks you do are practically unimportant. Real progress becomes evident when you shift your attention to the vital 20-percent.

• What you choose to not do is as important as what you choose to do.

• Most capable people are held back by the belief that all opportunities are equal and everything is important.

CHAPTER 4: TRADE-OFF: Which Problem Do I Want?

Southwest Airlines has consistently offered the best return on investment among the S&P 500 companies since 1972. The key to this success has been the pursuit of a strategy that involves making deliberate trade-offs. To cut costs, the airline focuses on offering point-on-point flights, offering nothing but coach services, and serving no meals onboard. While the company risks alienating customers who prefer the services it doesn't offer, Southwest makes these trade-offs because it is clear about the one thing it wants to be: a low-cost airline.

"You have to look at every opportunity and say, 'Well, no ... I'm sorry. We're not going to do a thousand different things that really won't contribute much to the end result we are trying to achieve.' "

A sustainable strategy is one that makes clear trade-offs in competing positions. When a company says it values competing ideals or groups of customers equally, it leaves the people tasked with implementing the strategy with no clear directive on what to do when they face competing positions. Even at a personal level, one must say no to several alternatives to adequately deliver on one project or opportunity.

Trade-offs are hard to make because they involve choosing from among things that one equally wants. While the nonessentialist asks how he can work on all the options he has, the essentialist knows he can't deliver equally on alternatives and chooses the problem he wants. He asks what he wants to go big on – rather than what he wants to sacrifice – and channels his energies towards achieving this one thing.

Key Takeaways

• Trade-offs represent opportunities in that they force you to select the best alternative and, by so doing, increase the chances of achieving the desired outcome.

• The essentialist recognizes that trade-offs are an inherent part of everything he does and so makes them deliberately and strategically.

PART II: EXPLORE

Discern the Vital Few from the Trivial Many

The essentialist explores numerous options and commits to a few important ones. The nonessentialist explores fewer options, gets excited at the prospect of achieving each of these options, and reacts to everything.

While the nonessentialist sees playing, sleeping, listening, and carving space to think, reflect and select as a waste of time, the essentialist knows these activities are vital for discerning what is vital. He knows that being overly busy is a poor metric for productivity.

CHAPTER 5: ESCAPE: The Perks of Being Unavailable

It is difficult to figure out what is important when you are always busy. Clarity and innovation come to you when you give yourself space and time to breathe, look around, and think. While the nonessentialist reacts to the needs of his environment and jumps on opportunities as they come, the essentialist deliberately creates time to explore and think and, subsequently, gets perspective on what is truly important.

The essentialist realizes that exploring and focusing are not things he does in passing; they are things he needs to escape to do. He turns off his electronics, cancels his appointments, and escapes to a secluded place where he is free to think and explore hundreds of possibilities.

Paradoxically, it is the people who are too busy to escape and reflect that need to escape the most. Only by stepping back – for an hour or more each day, as a continuous stretch of time or over small periods – can they understand why their schedules are running out of control. Creating space to read, analyzing trends, and thinking about the bigger picture are as important as pausing to reflect. Reading – especially inspirational classics – can take you back and force you to rethink what truly matters.

Key Takeaways

• Creating time to think and explore allows you to identify your highest point of contribution and take control of the use of your time.

CHAPTER 6: LOOK: See What Really Matters

The mark of good journalism is not to merely find and present the *who, what, why* and *when*; it is to understand what something means and why it matters and to present it from this perspective. As in life, there is always something hidden in a story or an event. Figuring out the relationship between the components of a story (or data, or information) is crucial to finding your highest point of contribution. By focusing too much on the details, you miss the bigger picture that would have made all the difference.

While the nonessentialist considers – and is often overwhelmed – by all the information he gets, the essentials knows that he can't pay attention to everything and so focuses on what is not being said. He pays attention only to the essence of the information he gets and filters the noise to get the bigger picture.

To ensure the essence of your life is always within view,

• Keep a daily journal and review it every three months or so. As you review your entries, focus on the trends of your life, not the details.

• Go out into the field to explore the problem, understand the real challenge, and recognize where you can make a meaningful difference.

• Look for a different perspective on a problem you face by gathering information about its context and relationship with other problems and putting yourself in the shoes of the main participants.

• Clarify the goals you want to accomplish and make a plan of action.

Key Takeaways

• To find your highest point of contribution, gather information about the work or problem at hand, explore the relationship between the pieces of information you have, and focus on what everything leads to.

CHAPTER 7: PLAY: Embrace the Wisdom of Your Inner Child

Play is as important for adults as it is for children; it encourages exploration and sparks creativity. Research has shown that play – defined as anything one does for its own sake – can improve personal relationships, health, productivity, and an organization's ability to innovate. While the nonessentialist thinks play is a triviality and a waste of time, the essentialist recognizes that play is crucial in developing his adaptability and awakening his creative genius.

Play invites exploration by bringing to view a wide range of possibilities, reducing stress (which inhibits creativity), and improving the executive functions of the brain – planning, analyzing, deciding, among others. Most of the breakthroughs in science and art were made by people at play.

Increasingly, innovative companies are promoting playfulness by decorating their physical environments with fun figures, making use of desk toys, and even initiating comedy classes, as is the case at Twitter.

Key Takeaways

• Play is essential in developing a creative, flexible, and adaptable mind. It is essential not just as a means to an end but in and of itself.

• Incorporate play into your work routine by recalling and recreating the things or activities that excited you as a child.

CHAPTER 8: SLEEP: Protect the Asset

It's easy for an overachiever – or anyone with boundless ambition – to forget that the best asset he has for making a contribution in the world is himself. Underinvesting in one's body, mind, and spirit undermines any effort made towards progress. Going without sufficient sleep is the mark of a person who doesn't pace himself. For this person, early burnout is always lurking around the corner.

While the nonessentialist sees sleep as a waste of time and an enemy of productivity, the essentialist understands that sleep – a full eight hours each night – is essential for improving performance. Without enough sleep, it becomes harder to think or see the bigger picture. The essentialist considers sleep a priority because it builds his creativity and problem solving skills. He purposely schedules sleep into his daily plan and chooses to sacrifice what he has to do during his sleep time so he can do more tomorrow.

Sleep is especially important for mastery because it allows a person working on his craft to do more. In a study of violists, Anders Ericsson found that the best violists spent more time practicing than their peers. The other significant factor that set them above their peers was sleep; they slept an average of 8.6 hours each night and took a nap of 2.8 hours each afternoon. Sleep rested their bodies and minds and, subsequently, allowed them to practice with greater concentration.

Key Takeaways

• Sleep allows you to reach your highest point of contribution by increasing your energy, concentration, creativity, and your ability to solve problems and discern what is important. It empowers you to achieve more in less time.

CHAPTER 9: SELECT: The Power of Extreme Criteria

Derek Sivers urges his readers to become more selective in the choices they make by using extreme criteria to evaluate decisions. If your response to a choice is not "Hell Yeah!" then it's a plain and simple "No." There is no in-between; there is no "Yes." A closet organizer doesn't ask you if there is a chance you will wear an article of clothing someday; he asks if you *absolutely* love a jacket or a pair of shoes you don't want to throw out. This approach sums up the choice philosophy of the essentialist.

You can use the 90-percent rule to make any decision or settle any dilemma you face. If you have a set of options and the option with the most important criteria you use to make a decision scores 100 percent, anything that scores less than 90 percent is not up for consideration. Using extreme criteria requires you to acknowledge that trade-offs – no matter how difficult they are to make – set you on course to realize the best outcome.

While it's easy to give in to convenient opportunities that don't fully meet your 90-percent criteria – partly due to the fear of missing out –, you risk having to let meaningful rewards go every time you choose easy rewards. Saying no to opportunities that are merely good even when you don't have any other offer on the table is the price you pay for choosing to be distinct and pursuing the bigger picture.

Key Takeaways

• Extreme criteria strip away the noise that accompanies choices and force you to think rationally and choose what is most essential.

• Using selective and explicit criteria in decision making epitomizes the essentialist's goal of "less but better."

PART III: ELIMINATE

How Can We Cut Out the Trivial Many?

It's not nearly enough to differentiate the vital few from the trivial many; you must get past the resistance of letting go (and the fear of "what if") and cut out nonessential activities to operate at your highest point of contribution. It is worth noting that the fear of letting go, even that which is clearly trivial, is normal. Studies have shown that people tend to value what they have more than it is worth, hence the difficulty of letting go. Still, the mark of the essentialist is his ability to evaluate competing priorities and say "no" to those that do not serve his purpose.

CHAPTER 10: CLARIFY: One Decision that Makes a Thousand

Since clarity of purpose is one of the chief determinants of success in any field, it is not enough to be "pretty clear" about your objectives. You must be "really clear" to direct your energies to the essential and eliminate the nonessential.

"When there is a serious lack of clarity about what the team stands for and what their goals and roles are, people experience confusion, stress, and frustration. When there is a high level of clarity, on the other hand, people thrive."

Whenever a purpose is unclear, a team loses sight of the bigger picture and wastes resources on trivial activities. As lack of clarity becomes manifest, team efforts are either redirected to playing politics or pursuing individual short-term interests. Even on a personal level, lack of clarity about your purpose in life pushes you to overvalue nonessentials like outward appearances, material gains, and trivialities like the number of reactions you get on a social media post.

To achieve clarity in your team or personal pursuits, start by identifying an essential intent. Unlike a vision (which is inspirational but too general) or a value (which is vague and general), an essential intent is inspirational and concrete. It is also meaningful and measurable and can eliminate a thousand future decisions if crafted well. Martha Lane Fox's description of her "Digital

Champion" campaign exemplifies an essential intent that is inspiring, concrete, and easily measurable. The campaign's intent is "To get everyone in the U.K online by the end of 2012." The intent brought clarity to Fox's team and offered a solid basis for discerning what activities or ideas were truly essential.

To develop a clear, concrete, and inspiring statement of purpose for your team, career, or personal life:

• Look past the words you have to include in your statement and focus on the substance. Start by finding out the one thing you can do exceptionally well.

• Ask yourself how you will know you have succeeded in your quest and incorporate the metric in the statement.

Key Takeaways

• To assess the true value of an opportunity (or anything you have), ask yourself what you would be willing to do to get it if you didn't have it.

• Clarity of purpose enables individuals, teams, and organizations to eliminate the false priorities that distract them from their purpose and make their highest contributions.

CHAPTER 11: DARE: The Power of a Graceful "No"

The most important – and the most difficult – skill an individual must muster to become an essentialist is the ability to say "no" with courage and grace. While it may seem that the difficulty of saying "no" stems from a fear of missing out – or the fear of disappointing someone you admire or respect – most people find it hard to turn down requests because they have not defined what is essential to them. Clarity offers a strong defense against the temptation to do the nonessential.

It is also difficult to say "no" because human beings are biologically wired to get along with others. Still, it pays to be clear about the choice: to say "no" and endure the social awkwardness and physical discomfort that comes with it for a few minutes, or say "yes" and regret the decision for the period it takes to complete the request.

Whereas the nonessentialist says yes to avoid the social awkwardness that comes with saying no, the essentialist knows that he has to endure the discomfort of saying no to focus and excel in what truly matters. He knows that he cannot please everyone, that saying yes to the nonessential will force him to sacrifice the essential, and that people respect him more when he resolutely says no.

To learn to say no gracefully:

• Understand that your relationship is separate from your decision; denying the request does not imply you are denying the person.

• Realize that there are many ways of refusing a request without actually saying no.

• Think about what you will have to give up if you accept the request.

• Remember that everyone is pushing for their agenda at the expense of your time.

• Understand that saying no may erode your popularity in the short-term but it earns you respect over the long run.

• Remember that a firm no is more settling (for the person who makes the request) than a noncommittal yes.

Some graceful ways to say no include: pausing to consider the request, saying what you are currently busy with (and asking to consider the request when you are done), asking to check your calendar first, and using email bouncebacks. Alternatively, you can counter the request with what you are willing to do – something that won't take as much of your time or resources – or suggest someone else who can help. If dealing with a superior who is difficult to say no to, ask him/her what you should deprioritize to take on the new request.

Key Takeaways

• Your effectiveness hinges on your ability to say no.

• When you say no firmly but gracefully, you realize that your mind exaggerated the fear of rejecting the request and find that people respect you more for your conviction.

CHAPTER 12: UNCOMMIT: Win Big by Cutting Your Losses

People tend to invest more resources in a losing project in the hope that they will recoup what they have already lost. While the nonessentialist refuses to admit his mistakes and keeps trying in the hope that something will work out in the end, the essentialist considers what he could do with the resources he is pouring into a losing project and cuts his losses early.

Apart from this sunk-cost bias, other common traps you need to avoid to keep sight of what really matters include:

The endowment effect. People tend to overvalue things they own or the activities they take part in and undervalue things or activities they don't own. To uncommit from the nonessential activities you own:

• Instead of asking how it would feel to miss out on your current commitment, ask yourself what you would be willing to do to get the opportunity if you didn't have it.

• Accept that only by admitting failure and letting go can you move on to success.

• Let go of the things that don't match your abilities to avoid wasting more resources.

• Get a second opinion about your fit for a project from a neutral party.

Status quo bias. People tend to blindly follow systems or commitments because they are already established. To overcome this bias:

• When you plan your schedule, assume you have no existing commitments and begin from scratch. Zero-based scheduling allows you to objectively assess whether an activity is worth the time and resources you are going to put in.

• Take time to consider before committing to casual requests.

The fear of missing out. This fear stems from a deep-rooted human need to avoid loss. To curb this fear:

• Scale back or eliminate any activity you think is essential – for just a few days – and note if there is any difference in your life or the people it concerns.

Key Takeaways

• Limit the energy and resources you lose in stalling projects or nonessential activities by challenging your cognitive biases.

CHAPTER 13: EDIT: The Invisible Art

A good editor makes it difficult to see anything but the important parts of a piece of art. He takes out the nonessential and leaves only what must be there. When you explore and distinguish the vital few from the trivial many, the next challenge you have to overcome to become an essentialist is to edit your life and responsibilities.

A good editor considers a thousand things he could leave in a story and looks for the intersection of a few of them. Out of these, he retains one or two things that are truly important. Paradoxically, a good editor deliberately subtracts items to add life to the core ideas. As in a professional capacity, disciplined personal editing removes the unnecessary to focus energy on what is essential and increase contribution. This subtraction involves significant trade-offs; you must learn to kill your darlings if they don't make your story better – even if they took years to develop.

To edit nonessentials from your life:

Cut out options. Having fewer options reduces the mental resources you need to make a decision. Cut out any option that is merely good.

Condense. Replace multiple meaningless activities with a few meaningful ones to lower the ratio of efforts to results.

Correct. Refer to your ultimate purpose to correct activities that are not in line with your intent.

Edit less. Practice restraint; wait, observe, and resist the urge to jump into things that come your way.

Key Takeaways

• The goal of becoming an editor of your life is to rid your life of trivialities and distractions so you can focus on what truly matters.

• For the essentialist, editing is a continuous process that involves cutting out options to ease decision making, condensing meaningless activities like meetings to make room for important activities, and correcting parts of a daily routine that are not in line with the ultimate intent.

CHAPTER 14: LIMIT: The Freedom of Setting Boundaries

It is not so much that the boundary between work and family has been blurred in the nonessentialist era; it is work that has slowly crept into family territory. Having unclear boundaries sets you on a slippery path where you consent to requests you would not have otherwise considered – like attending a work meeting on Sunday. When you give in once, you are bound to give in again.

"Boundaries are a little like the walls of a sandcastle. The second we let one fall over, the rest of them come crashing down."

Setting and sticking to strict boundaries is difficult because it comes with an inherent risk. For example, refusing requests because they violate your boundaries could limit the opportunities you get. However, the cost of not pushing back is often higher: the line between the essential and nonessential fades with every boundary that breaks.

Since nonessentialists think they can handle everything, they view boundaries as constraints to their productivity. However, the lack of boundaries stretches their time and energy so much that completing anything becomes a challenge. Essentialists know that boundaries are important tools for protecting time and limiting the temptation to work on the nonessential requests made by other people. Boundaries that other people are aware of eliminate the need to keep saying no and keep you from working on what not essential to your purpose.

When you don't set limits, other people imprison you with the limits they set for you. Paradoxically, putting up fences around what you can and can't do frees you to explore all the options you choose to include within your fence. Consider this analogy: children playing near a busy road may limit their movement to a small safe space set by their supervisors. If a fence is erected around the playground, the children are free to move around the entire expanse of the grounds, even the areas near the road.

To set clear limits and to ensure people respect them, find your deal breakers and make them clear to the people you interact with. Any request you refuse or any invitation that you feel violates your independence or priorities is a potential deal breaker. At the start of a project, make your priorities known and be assertive about the extra work that you can or can't take.

Key Takeaways

• Without clear boundaries, other people's agendas/problems easily become your agenda/problem.

• Setting limits does not limit you; it frees you to do all the things that matter to you.

PART IV: EXECUTE

How to Make Execution Effortless

Essentialists design systems that eliminate nonessential activities or commitments and, subsequently, make the execution of the things that matter effortless. Because nonessentialists lack this system, they have to force execution every day.

CHAPTER 15: BUFFER: The Unfair Advantage

In the face of constant change, you can either react to every unforeseen circumstance that comes your way or prepare for the unexpected by creating a buffer. A buffer is anything that prevents two items or activities from crashing by creating space between them.

Buffers are essential at work and home because projects, like gases, tend to expand to fill the space available. A buffer allows you to focus on what you have to do. It limits the need to rush at the last minute to accommodate things you have to complete. While the nonessentialist bets on best-case scenarios and underestimates the time it takes to complete activities, the essentialist knows something unexpected almost always happens and makes early preparations.

To limit friction between the essential things you have to do:

• **Use extreme preparation.** Prepare well in advance for anything that can go wrong, no matter how improbable.

• **Add 50 percent to your time estimate.** To limit the constant danger of underestimating the time it takes to complete a project, add a 50-percent buffer to the time you estimate. If you estimate it will take you twenty minutes to get to a meeting, leave for the meeting thirty minutes before it begins.

• **Conduct scenario planning.** For each important project, assess the risks you face, the worst-case scenario, and the social and financial impact of each scenario. Determine the areas you can invest in to reduce the risks.

Key Takeaways

• The essentialist knows things rarely go according to plan; he anticipates the unexpected and creates buffers to reduce the friction created by unexpected events.

CHAPTER 16: SUBTRACT: Bring Forth More by Removing Obstacles

A manager with good insight knows that he only needs to find the obstacle holding a system back to turn around the entire organization. If he improves everything else but fails to address the main constraint, the overall change will be dismal. In the same way, only by finding and removing the *biggest* obstacle from your system – be it a project, department, or personal relationship – can you make the highest contribution in your work or life.

The essentialist views progress as a game of subtraction rather than addition; he knows that he can achieve more, not by doing more, but by removing more obstacles. To find and address the constraints holding back your system:

• **Clarify your essential intent.** Only by having a clear view of where you are going can you see the stumbling blocks along the way.

• **Identify the biggest obstacle.** Take some time to think about the major things keeping you from completing your project. Find the obstacle that is the source of other obstacles.

• **Remove the obstacle.** Start with the primary obstacle and work your way through smaller obstacles.

Key Takeaways

• Find and remove the biggest constraints from your system to expedite your progress. Fixing immediate or arbitrary obstacles only produces marginal improvements.

CHAPTER 17: PROGRESS: The Power of Small Wins

While the nonessentialist tries to increase his contribution by going big on everything he does, the essentialist knows that the more he strives, the harder it becomes to achieve anything. He knows that big goals become burdensome soon enough and are easy to abandon. Instead, the essentialist makes small steps in essential areas to realize simple wins that add up over time. By realizing and celebrating these small wins, he builds the motivation to do more.

"Research has shown that of all forms of human motivation the most effective one is progress. Why? Because a small, concrete win creates momentum and affirms our faith in our further success."

Starting 'early and small' builds the momentum that enables the essentialist to accomplish a goal without friction. The key is to start by making the minimum time investment at the earliest time possible. If it's a project that takes months, the essentialist takes a few minutes – as early on as possible – to come up with some ideas before moving on to something else.

Key Takeaways

• Instead of forcing a big win and burning out in the process, create small wins to build the momentum you need to make more wins.

• Make a visual representation of the progress you are making towards your goal to keep your motivation alive.

CHAPTER 18: FLOW: The Genius of Routine

The nonessentialist thinks one must force execution and apply raw effort to accomplish the things that matter. The essentialist makes execution effortless by including his most important tasks in a routine that he practices over and over until it becomes his default position. He realizes that in addition to easing execution, routine undermines the pull of nonessential activities.

Routine increases productivity by freeing up the mental resources you need to concentrate. With the freed up mental resources, you can concentrate on new activities while being actively engaged in the other activity and without compromising quality. Essentially, routine enables the brain to work less and less. The saved energy fosters innovation and creativity and eliminates the need to make the same decisions over and over again.

The challenge that comes with routine is to avoid getting caught up in nonessential habits. You can replace your nonessential habits with routines that work for you by doing the following:

• **Overhaul your triggers.** Identify the cue that triggers your unwanted habit and associate it with essential behavior. For example, if your alarm clock cues you to check your social media pages whenever it goes off, use the cue to plan your schedule instead. Over time, the relationship between the cue (alarm clock) and the new behavior (planning) strengthens and forms a new habit.

• **Create new triggers.** Use a cue for an established habit as the cue for the habit you want to form. Keeping your journal near your phone can cue you to write a few lines each time you reach for your phone.

• **Start with the most difficult task.** Free up the mental resources you need for the day (and the willpower you need to execute essential activities) by working on the hardest task first thing in the morning.

• **Mix up routines.** Develop different routines for different days to avoid routine fatigue. Trying tying up each day's routine in a central theme.

• **Start small.** Start with one change and develop a routine over it before moving to something else.

Key Takeaways

• When you make the pursuit of the essential part of your routine, you achieve it effortlessly.

CHAPTER 19: FOCUS: What's Important Now?

Asking yourself what is the most important thing now keeps you present and focused on what matters and, subsequently, makes execution effortless. Finding and deliberately tuning in to the most important task of the moment undermines the tendency to get caught up in what went wrong in the past or what has to happen in the future and allows you to focus on *how* you execute the current task. Every moment you spend worrying about the past or feeling anxious about the future distracts you from what you have to do here and now.

To become fully present on everything you do:

• **Figure out the most important thing right now.** Make a list of the things you feel you should be doing and use the 90-percent rule to find what is most important.

• **Get the future out of your head.** There is only Now. Make a list of the things you want to do in future to rid you mind of the distraction.

• **Prioritize.** Work through your list of essential tasks and cross each item when it's complete.

Key Takeaways

• Like a nonessentialist, the essentialist knows he can multitask. The difference is that the essentialist knows he can't multi-focus.

• When dealing with multiple obligations or distractions, the most important thing is to figure out the most important thing.

CHAPTER 20: BE: The Essentialist Life

Essentialism is not something you add to your life or do occasionally; it is a way of life that you adopt and become one with. It is a lifestyle – a way to do everything simply and differently. This lifestyle has deep roots in spiritual traditions and the lives of notable personalities. Gautama Buddha, Mahatma Gandhi, and Moses (who liberated the Israelites from Egypt) left their opulent lives behind to live simply pursue meaning, and make high contributions in the lives of others. The philosophy of "Less but better" is also notable in the lives of Mother Teresa, Warren Buffet, Steve Jobs, Leo Tolstoy, and the Dalai Lama.

People who are essentialists at their core may get caught up in nonessentials once in a while, but they get more from this lifestyle than people who adopt essentialism at the surface. Every step they make towards pursuing the essential builds up on itself, and the sway of frivolities grows thinner and thinner. As you practice each essentialist ideal, the essentialist lifestyle becomes instinctive and changes you.

Becoming an essentialist may take years of practice, but its benefits are undeniable. It comes with more clarity about what really matters, more control over time and choices, and more joy at the newfound fullness of life.

Key Takeaways

• To distinguish the necessary from the real, the major from the minor, is to simplify your life.

• Essentialism is about making few accomplishments that have meaning instead of having a long list of achievements that have little significance.

APPENDIX: Leadership Essentials

The leading predictor of success in organizational teams is clarity of purpose. When the goal of the team and the roles of each team member are unclear, confusion, stress and frustration set in and, ultimately, failure becomes inevitable. The philosophy of "less but better" is as important for teams as it is for individuals because it helps distinguish essential opportunities from ideas the team should not be wasting time on. By being selective on talent, strategy, individual contribution, and information, the essentialist leader creates a unified team and makes a million miles of progress in one direction rather than a millimeter of progress in a million directions.

END

SUMMARY
of
THE
CHECKLIST
MANIFESTO

How to Get Things Right

by Atul Gawande

*A FastReads Book Summary with
Key Takeaways & Analysis*

EXECUTIVE SUMMARY

In this book, Atul Gawande explores the growing complexity of the world and offers a straightforward and universal solution: a checklist. He argues that most problems—whether experienced in the intensity of the surgical ward or the fiery kitchen of a world-class restaurant—are preventable and only require simple, cheap, and transmissible solutions. The checklist is the last line of defense in the fight against an unmanageable body of knowledge, distractions, and faulty memory.

Gawande draws from his experiences as a surgeon and from the experiences of professionals in the aviation, construction, and finance industry to present a compelling argument for the adoption of this effective yet overlooked tool. He reveals how industries can leverage the power of the checklist and increase the uptake of new knowledge, ease decision making, and increase efficiency by condensing information into a usable and systematic form.

INTRODUCTION

The shock of the unexpected can have dire consequences, especially where a project or a life depends on having everything under control. In one incidence, a general surgeon in San Francisco almost lost a patient with a stab wound because no one thought to ask the patient or the emergency personnel what weapon the attacker used. Had the surgeon known earlier on that the weapon used was a bayonet; he would not have taken his time or treated the wound as a superficial injury.

People fail primarily because the things they try to accomplish are beyond their understanding, their immediate control, or their physical and mental powers. For things that are within control, people may still fail because of their ignorance—described here as limited understanding due to gaps in knowledge—or ineptitude, described as failure to apply available knowledge correctly. In the past few decades, the human race has made unprecedented breakthroughs in almost all spheres of life. Increasing knowledge has meant that ineptitude is, for the first time in history, a more probable cause of failure than ignorance.

Failures in medical institutions are not so much a consequence of insufficient funding or government interference as they are a result of the increasing complexity of science and the subsequent difficulty of applying new knowledge correctly and consistently. Increasing ineptitude is not a preserve of the medical field; it is also evident in software design, law and governance, finance, and just about any other field that deals with vast knowledge and requires mastery.

Avoidable failures are frequent in these fields because the available know-how is rapidly becoming unmanageable.

"The volume and complexity of what we know has exceeded our individual ability to deliver its benefits correctly, safely, or reliably. Knowledge has both saved us and burdened us."

For these avoidable failures, the remedy—as simplistic as it may sound—is a checklist.

Key Takeaways

• The challenge of the 21st century is not lack of sufficient knowledge to solve complex problems; it is the inability to manage and apply increasing know-how.

• Avoidable failure is the bane of most professions today because the complex body of knowledge available is proving to be too much for the fallible human memory to handle.

CHAPTER 1: THE PROBLEM OF EXTREME COMPLEXITY

Resuscitating a drowning victim who has been underwater for thirty minutes and lifeless for two hours is as complex as any medical procedure can get. Each step involved is immensely difficult, and every incision, every heart-lung bypass, must be made in the right sequence. Indeed, medicine has evolved from the conventional science where penicillin was the magical cure-all for infectious diseases to a contemporary art where success depends on how well the surgeon, clinician, or nurse manages complexity. However, with more than thirteen thousand different ways the body can fail; and with each disease, syndrome and injury type requiring different considerations and procedures, mastery seems like a superhuman endeavor.

As scientists discover new genetic disorders, diagnoses, and treatment procedures almost every week, the complexity of medical practice is growing so rapidly that information systems—let alone the practitioners—are struggling to keep up. Even then, with all its complexity, new knowledge is necessary to lower the odds of error and raise the rates of survival.

To cope with the pressure of increasing complexity, practitioners have gone from being specialists to being superspecialists. The author, for example, has gone from being a general surgeon to specializing in surgical oncology to specializing even further in endocrine cancer surgery. The effect of superspecialization has been a remarkable improvement in the capability and success of medical procedures.

However, even with this success, at least half of the major complications and fatalities that occur in surgery have been marked as avoidable. Expertise and superspecialization, it would seem, are just not enough.

Key Takeaways

• Specialization—and in extension, superspecialization—are hardly enough to ensure professionals correctly and consistently apply the wide base of knowledge available in their fields.

CHAPTER 2: THE CHECKLIST

On October 30, 1935, Boeing Model 299 crashed shortly after taking off, killing two of the five crew members taking part in the test flight, including a seasoned pilot. An investigation into the crash revealed that the pilot had simply forgotten to release a locking mechanism on the rudder and elevator controls. With four engines—each requiring its own fuel mix—and a host of tabs that needed adjusting, the plane had too many things for one pilot to handle.

Boeing's response to the incident that almost bankrupted the company was not to take the model's pilots through additional training; it was to develop a brief and simple list with step-by-step checks for each action required for takeoff, flight, and landing. While the checklist did not have anything new—it comprised of the mundane checks pilots always made—it enabled the pilots to fly the Model 299 for nearly two million miles without any incidence.

Most of what lawyers, clinicians, financial managers, and software engineers do today is too complex to execute from memory. Most professional fields simply have too much for one person to handle. A checklist may sound simplistic, especially for clinicians who have to handle thousands of different conditions. But the vital signs nurses check for every hospital record such as pulse, respiratory rate, blood pressure, and body temperature make up a simple yet indispensable checklist.

In complex environments, faulty memory combined with the strain or distractions of the job can easily cause an expert to skip a key step in a process. In processes where missing one step has the same consequence as missing all steps—as is the case in preparing a plane for takeoff or checking a patient's vitals—entire projects and lives can hang in the balance. Even when he remembers to perform every check, the relative unimportance of one step may lure an expert to skip it. Checklists guard against the consequences of faulty memory and mitigate the temptation to overlook steps that don't always matter.

In 2001, nurses at Johns Hopkins Hospital inspired a critical care specialist at the hospital to develop a checklist for central line infections. Within a year, the infection rate among patients in the hospital's ICU had gone from 11 percent to zero. After developing more checklists for the ICU, the specialist found that the tool—which most doctors brush off as a triviality given their years of training—reduced the average time patients spent in the ICU by half.

Key Takeaways

• Checklists provide a safeguard against failure arising from faulty memory, distractions, and intentionally skipped steps.

• Checklists ease verification and encourage consistent and high standards of performance by reminding professionals of the minimum necessary steps in a process.

CHAPTER 3: THE END OF THE MASTER BUILDER

Checklists limit the prevalence and consequences of flaws in attention, memory, and thoroughness. Among experienced people, checklists guard against failure from unexpected sources. Still, checklists, like every other tool, have their limits and are only useful for solving certain types of problems.

Simple problems, like baking a cake, can be solved by following steps on a recipe. Complicated problems, like launching a rocket, comprise of a series of simple problems. Unlike simple problems, these problems do not have a straightforward recipe. They require teams and specialized expertise to solve. All the same, experts can build off the success of one project because rockets are largely similar. On the other hand, complex problems like raising a child have no recipe or definite outcome and are difficult to perfect even with experience as each child is different.

Preventing the Boeing crash of 1935 and stopping infections in the ICU are simple problems because the contributing factors in each of these problems are simple and can be solved simply by paying attention. Most professions often deal with simple problems such as a lawyer forgetting a critical line of defense in a fraud case, or a policeman forgetting to inform a suspect his rights. However, for professions that deal with critical work, a checklist may not be of much use. Clinicians, for example, cannot have a checklist for each of the 178 tasks they have to perform in the ICU. For complex problems, following judgment may produce better outcomes than following procedure.

The success of complex projects comes down to two things: ascertaining project owners have the right knowledge and making certain they apply it correctly. The conventional approach to achieving this has been to specialize in a few domains and limit external interference in one's work. Throughout most of history, master builders oversaw construction from inception to end, passing their knowledge only to the people who needed it. In recent years, the complexity of each stage of construction has become too much for any one person to master. Increasing complexity has marked the death of the all-knowing expert.

For a major construction, the project executive has to ensure that each of the five hundred or so workers does his specialized work correctly. With numerous considerations to make, and with insufficient knowledge of the nuances of most of the worker's tasks, the executive uses checklists to ensure the building comes together properly.

A schedule of each of the tasks that workers need to accomplish each day is the executive's best chance for maintaining order. Representatives from each of the sixteen or so trades involved in the construction draw up the checklist. The executive is responsible for ensuring workers complete each item on the checklist before they begin working on the next task. Essentially, the checklist ensures the knowledge of hundreds of stakeholders is employed in the right place, at the right time, and in the right way.

To deal with uncertainty, which is inevitable in complex ventures, a project executive maintains a submittal schedule. This schedule is a checklist that details communication tasks for experts in stages where something could go wrong. The team of experts meets on each day marked on the schedule to discuss a potential problem or unplanned development and submit their knowledge to the workers before the next stage commences. Although buildings are more complex than they were three decades ago, they take less time to build and are safer today because structural engineers have harnessed the power of checklists.

Key Takeaways

• Most of the problems people face are simple and require artless and straightforward solutions like checklists.

• Checklists ensure the knowledge of experts and stakeholders is put to proper use in the right place and at the right time.

• Anything can go wrong in a complex project. While a master builder is fallible, a team of experts with a checklist can identify and avert serious problems.

CHAPTER 4: THE IDEA

Checklists, especially those used in construction sites, outline critical steps and ensure that the people tasked with implementing a project complete it exactly the way the project owners wanted.

The best way to solve non-routine problems and tasks—as demonstrated by the submittal schedule—is to take power away from the center and distribute it among people with experience and expertise. While conventional checklists work well with routine tasks, shared responsibility and effective communication are the keys to solving complex and unexpected problems. Building inspectors use this approach: they ensure project owners have the proper checks in place and distribute power and responsibility by making builders sign affidavits stating that they have followed the codes.

For situations that are truly complex, efforts to force instructions from a central authority fail because the knowledge needed is beyond the scope of a single party and conditions change too unexpectedly for isolated individuals to keep up. When Hurricane Katrina hit New Orleans in 2005, federal, state, and local officials argued over who had the power to make decisions and disseminate resources as conditions deteriorated. Buses for evacuating people and trucks with supplies were refused entry into the state for days simply because authorities could not disperse power to the periphery.

Lee Scott, the then CEO of Wal-Mart, made the best response to the catastrophe by disseminating power and responsibility. As the company prepared to deal with the disaster which had forced the closure of 126 of its stores and displaced thousands of its employees and their families, Scott told a team of managers:

"A lot of you are going to have to make decisions above your level. Make the best decision that you can with the information that's available to you at the time, and, above all, do the right thing."

With this decision, upper management empowered store managers to devise creative solutions to get their stores running again and to use their best judgment to distribute supplies in the worst-hit areas. As they did this, the

Federal Emergency Management Agency was still struggling to figure things out.

The building industry has mastered complex situations by codifying freedom and discipline into a checklist. The industry makes certain that the balance between specialized ability and group collaboration works by using checklists: one for routine autonomous tasks and one for communication. These checklists ensure nothing is overlooked and people and coordinate their efforts.

Checklists have ensured that nothing goes horribly wrong for rock bands like Van Halen that have tons of equipment and hundreds of ways promoters could screw things up. Checklists have also proved vital for world-class restaurants that have to serve ever-evolving food while maintaining an extraordinary level of excellence. As checklists, recipes are vital tools for ensuring that quality remains consistent over time. Experienced chefs may not like the idea of using recipes, but it's when a chef believes she has everything under control that things begin to slip.

Key Takeaways

• Authorities that refuse to disperse their power and responsibility become inefficient as they struggle to keep up with the complex body of knowledge needed to make decisions. For these authorities, failure is inevitable.

• Owners of complex projects can maximize chances of success by using simple checklists for routine tasks and communication checklists for unexpected occurrences.

CHAPTER 5: THE FIRST TRY

In 2006, the World Health Organization contacted Gawande to help organize a meeting of healthcare stakeholders who would devise solutions for reducing avoidable deaths and harm from surgery. The task seemed impossible; with more than 25,000 different surgical procedures, reducing harm in every surgical unit across the globe would require efforts of unprecedented scale.

In January 2007, Gawande attended the two-day meeting in Geneva alongside other surgeons, nurses, clinicians, safety experts, and patients from around the world. The aim was to propose measures to reduce serious complications rates that ranged between 5 and 15 percent in hospital operations. The committee found that, in places like the United States, half of these complications were preventable. The committee also found that efforts to reduce these complications—including the introduction of incentive schemes and additional training programs—had only produced marginal results.

After analyzing public health programs around the world—from the smallpox vaccination campaign that eradicated polio in 1979 to the closure of a public well that ended the London cholera outbreak of 1854—Gawande found that effective solutions to complex health problems were simple, measurable, and transmissible. He found that in a year-long experiment in the crowded slums of Karachi, the proper use of soap alone had reduced the incidence of diarrhea among children by 52 percent. People in Karachi already used soap; it was the cleaning guidelines that came with the soaps that made most of the difference.

Gawande reviewed checklists that surgeons used to reduce harm at the Columbus Children's Hospital, Johns Hopkins Hospital, and the University of Toronto Hospital. All the checklists followed the same design and had been significantly successful in mitigating three of the four surgical killers: infection, bleeding, and unsafe anesthesia. The hospitals anticipated the fourth killer—unexpected complications—by requiring the surgical unit to pause and talk about the potential dangers of each patient at least a minute before starting an operation.

Teamwork is a crucial component of any effort to address unexpected outcomes. It is not the arrogance of experts that sinks the ship; it is their insistence to stick to their narrow domains and disregard the input of outsiders.

Whether at the surgical table or in the cockpit of large aircraft, experts and non-experts must work as a team to ensure nothing falls through the cracks.

As part of the checklist, the three hospitals also insisted that surgical members had to introduce themselves by name and role before starting any operation. This check encouraged a sort of camaraderie that dramatically improved communication and teamwork.

The WHO convention picked up the checklist idea as a viable solution. A working group condensed checklists that had been tried into three pauses: one before the administration of anesthesia, one before incision, and one after the operation. For each pause point, the group included checks for conditions, equipment, and anything that might be a potential source of harm. The group also included communication checks so surgical teams could become familiar with each member's name, role, and concerns before commencing the operation.

Gawande tried implementing the new checklist at his surgical unit when he got back from the WHO convention. However, he found it was too long and ambiguous and decided to abandon it.

Key Takeaways

• Effective solutions to complex problems have three attributes in common: they are simple, measurable, and transmissible.

• Checklists that are too long can easily distract the people making checks from the real work at hand.

CHAPTER 6: THE CHECKLIST FACTORY

After failing with the initial checklist, Gawande did some research to find out how flight checklists are made. He visited Boeing's headquarters in Seattle where he discovered that pilots had normal checklists for routine tasks like starting engines and taxiing and non-normal checklists for every emergency situation imaginable.

Daniel Boorman, a veteran pilot and Gawande's contact at the company, explained that bad checklists are long, vague, and imprecise: the product of people out of touch with the situations requiring the checklist. Good checklists are precise, practical, and easy to use. Instead of spelling out everything, they provide brief reminders of important steps that are easy to miss.

The value of checklists is limited by the fact that their implementation is the prerogative of the team. Luckily, aviation schools train pilots not to rely on their memory. Field experiences have also proved the value of checklists, so pilots have been apt to fish them out whenever there's an emergency.

To make a checklist, Boorman explained, one must first define the pause point: the natural point at which the team pauses to make checks. The drafter can choose between one of two checklists: a do-confirm checklist that people use to ensure what they did from memory is the right thing or a read-do checklist that people go through to know what they have to do next. Whatever the choice, the checklist has to be short because people get distracted when they check things off for more than a minute.

"The checklist cannot be lengthy. A rule of thumb some use is to keep it to between five and nine items, which is the limit of working memory."

Ideally, the checklist should fit on one page, be free of clutter, and be easy to read. The wording of the checklist has to be simple and exact to avoid confusion. The checklist must be tested in a practical setting for the drafters to see where it falls short and make changes. In the aviation industry, drafters test new checklists in flight simulators.

Pilots are able to stay up to date with new discoveries because when a thick and detailed crash investigation report comes out, people like Boorman shrink it to its practical essence and disseminate the new information in new or edited checklists.

Key Takeaways

• Checklists are not comprehensive guides detailing every step of a complex process; they are quick and simple tools that contain only the critical steps that are easy to overlook.

• In most professional fields, discoveries and corrective measures take long to implement because they come in bulletins with hundreds of pages. Translating knowledge into a simple and systematic form significantly increases the chances of implementation.

CHAPTER 7: THE TEST

When Gawande got back to Boston, he got his research team to make the Geneva checklist more usable by redrafting it into a clearer and shorter version. The team adopted a do-confirm format to give surgical units more flexibility in task execution. The checklist included three pause points for surgical procedures: before anesthesia, before making the first incision, and before leaving the operating room.

After redesigning the checklist, the team tested it in a simulation room with one of the assistants acting as the patient. The simulation revealed—among other issues—that the team had not specified who would be in charge of making the checks. Everyone agreed the circulating nurse could call the checks, and that she didn't have to make written check marks. The team also realized that it had to cut off non-killer items to reduce the time it took to make the checks to sixty seconds or less.

The WHO group considered these issues when it reconvened in the spring of 2007. The group decided to drop rare occurrences like operating room fires in favor of other pressing concerns like bleeding and infections. It left in checks for rare but controversial incidences like operating on the wrong patient because they took minimal time to make.

After making a few tests with the new checklist, the group made some brief changes and readied the final checklist for circulation. The final checklist had nineteen checks: seven before anesthesia (including confirming patient identity, consent, surgical site, and potential complications), seven before incision (introduction of team members, confirmation of patient and procedure, review of operation details), and five after the operation (labeling tissue specimens, accounting for all equipment used, and review of recovery concerns).

Gawande and his team lined up eight hospitals to take part in a test study of the effectiveness of the new surgery checklist. The hospitals selected were leading or intensely busy healthcare institutions in the United States, Canada, New Zealand, the United Kingdom, Philippines, Jordan, India, and Tanzania. Local research coordinators collected data from the surgical units of the eight hospitals three months prior to the introduction of the surgery checklist. The data revealed that the hospitals had complication rates of between 6 and 21 percent. Half of the complications involved infections and a quarter were a result of technical failures. In all the hospitals, teams missed some of the minimum steps involved in surgery while operating on two out of every three patients.

The hospitals recruited in the study began implementing the two-minute surgery checklist in the spring of 2008. Gawande's team got hospital leaders to take charge of the process and introduce the checklist gradually and systematically. Introducing the checklist in one operating room before issuing it to all surgical units allowed each hospital to make its own adjustments on the checklist.

At first, getting surgical teams to use the checklist proved to be challenging. Although the checklists were simple and straightforward, they were unwelcome because they represented yet another form of change that surgical units had to contend with. While some teams forgot some checks, others found that the checklist reversed established roles and caused some social uneasiness. All the same, the use of the checklist got well underway in all eight hospitals within the first month of its introduction.

The results, which came in October 2008, showed that major complications among patients in all eight locations had fallen by 36 percent since the introduction of the checklist. Returns to the operating room due to technical problems had fallen by a quarter, infections by half, and deaths by 47 percent. The results, which were published in the New England Journal of Medicine, motivated health stakeholders in the U.K and Washington State to campaign for the adoption of the checklist in their hospitals.

Key Takeaways

• By improving communication—especially by getting team members acquainted with each other's names and roles—checklists foster teamwork, increase efficiency, and reduce complications outside the scope of the checklist.

CHAPTER 8: THE HERO IN THE AGE OF CHECKLISTS

Since the publication of the results of the WHO surgery checklist, more than a dozen countries have made plans to implement the checklist in hospitals within their jurisdiction. By the end of 2009, more than two thousand hospitals around the world had implemented the checklist or were taking steps to implement it.

Still, the checklist has been slow to adopt partly because it is not a magical cure or flashy state-of-the art technology like surgical robots, and partly because its introduction in the operating room has been through a top-down approach. The belief that situations involving risk require an audacious expert to take charge has also undermined the willingness to adopt the checklist. Experts, it would seem, forget that a checklist does not take away the courage and inventiveness needed to handle complex procedures.

Teams can leverage the power of the checklist to do even more: they can make specialized checks for non-routine procedures or any processes that involve a level of uncertainty, risk, and complexity.

"Just ticking boxes is not the ultimate goal here. Embracing a culture of teamwork and discipline is. And if we recognize the opportunity, the two-minute WHO checklist is just a start."

Beyond medicine, the checklist offers opportunities for streamlining operations and limiting loss. In finance, for example, visionaries are using checklists to prevent the common investment mistakes that professionals make due to panic or irrational exuberance. Simple checks make analysis and investment decisions objective by ensuring that a team has gone through an investment's potential returns, industry outlook, and management record. In the absence of a checklist, emotions take over: bull markets lure the investor to take shortcuts and bear markets bring a wave of panic.

A written checklist accommodates all the features or patterns an investor needs to make sound decisions. Even for seasoned investors, some patterns are easy to miss when left to memory. The intelligent investor analyzes patterns of mistakes among his peers and accommodates them in his decision-making checklist to ensure he doesn't fall into the same trap. He goes even further and enumerates potential errors in research, decision making, execution, and monitoring. He condenses these errors into simple 'yes' or 'no' checks and adds them to his checklist. Each stage of the investment process becomes his pause point.

"The checklist doesn't tell him what to do... It is not a formula. But the checklist helps him be as smart as possible every step of the way, ensuring that he's got the critical information he needs when he needs it, that he's systematic about decision making, that he's talked to everyone he should."

Checklists offer an efficient way to weed out investments that are not worth lengthy investigations. Yet, most people refuse to use these checklists because they feel that their problem-solving abilities are too advanced for a simple tool to be of any help. They forget that checklists get dumb, but easily forgettable stuff, out of the way so they can focus on the vital stuff.

As knowledge grows and surpasses the handling capabilities of any one person, professionals need discipline; first to adhere to procedure when they have to and second to make reasonable improvisations when the situation calls for creative problem solving. Checklists foster this discipline. They ensure that the systems people depend on work. They are the last defenses against the complexity of the world.

Key Takeaways

• Any professional can make significant gains by looking for patterns of failure in his field and codifying them into simple and straightforward checks.

• By simply ensuring that the surgeon washes his hands, or that the investor goes through the footnotes of a company report to uncover hidden trends, a checklist improves outcomes without requiring an increase in skill.

• Checklists speed up decision making by making it more methodological.

CHAPTER 9: THE SAVE

When the initial checklist came out in 2007, Gawande didn't think it would make any difference in his surgical operations. He decided to try it all the same—if only to gauge its usability. He was surprised to find that over the period he used the checklist, his team caught mistakes every week. These mistakes, such as forgetting to administer antibiotics before surgery, would have been missed were it not for the checklist.

Gawande realized that while surgical operations were routine, patients and their conditions were not. The surgery checklist helped reduce the complexity of operating on different patients—each with special considerations—and catch drug allergies, medication errors, and mistakes on specimen labels. Left unaddressed, some of these mistakes could be fatal.

Gawande recalls that the checklist saved the life of a fifty-three-year-old man he was operating on to remove a cancerous adrenal gland. During the operation, Gawande made an accidental tear in the patient's vena cava: the artery returning blood to the heart. The tear caused unstoppable bleeding, and the patient went into cardiac arrest within sixty seconds. Earlier on, while going through the pre-surgery checks, Gawande had mentioned that significant blood loss was a potential concern in this type of surgery. The assisting nurse had set aside four units of blood to guard against this outcome.

The potential-concerns check saved the patient's life.

Key Takeaways

• A checklist may not prevent unexpected complications, but it ensures a team is ready to handle each complication as it arises.

END

SUMMARY
of
DESIGNING
YOUR LIFE

How to Build a Well-Lived, Joyful Life

by Bill Burnett & Dave Evans

A FastReads Book Summary with
Key Takeaways & Analysis

EXECUTIVE SUMMARY

In this book, Bill Burnett and Dave Evans reveal how anyone can use design thinking to answer some of life's most pressing questions: Why am I here, and what do I do with my life? The authors contend that just as design thinking has helped create complex bridges, sexy sports cars, and ultra-fast computers, its innovative principles can help create a meaningful and fulfilling life too. Anyone at any stage of their life or career can design the life they want by developing a beginner's mind, generating lots of options, prototyping viable ideas, and mustering the courage to live into the choices they make.

The authors draw from their wide base of knowledge as engineers and their experiences as instructors of a design course at Stanford to show how people can treat any problem as a design problem and develop innovative and workable solutions. They maintain that happiness and success are not things you stumble on by making the right choice; they are processes you create by choosing what energizes and feels true to you.

INTRODUCTION: LIFE BY DESIGN

Most people struggle to figure out what to do with their lives because some popular but dysfunctional beliefs prevent them from making the best of their circumstances. Some of the self-perpetuated myths that keep people from designing the careers and lives they want include:

1.The belief that you have to pursue a career related to your degree. Venturing outside your field of study is hardly an anomaly. Only about 27 percent of college graduates end up working in a field they majored in.

2.The belief that you will happy when you become successful. Happiness comes from creating a life that feels true and works for you. About two-thirds of workers in America – including high-flying professionals who are the very definition of success – are unhappy with their jobs because they are losing sight of this fact.

3.The belief that it's too late to find work that gives you meaning. It's never too late to design a joyful and meaningful career.

Designers love problems

Everything around you – from the furniture and electronics to the air conditioning system – was designed to solve a problem. Design thinking has solved some of the most pressing engineering problems: It has helped create complex bridges, high-performance computer hardware, and even the sexy aesthetics of sports cars. About everything that makes life easier and enjoyable was once a problem that someone solved with a design. You can create a life of meaning, joy, and fulfillment using the same design thinking.

Unlike the engineer designing a complex bridge, the life designer has no clear goal to work with and no hard data to help him choose the best design. Even with clear goals, data, and analysis, the solution does not easily come to the engineer or the life designer. Both have to improvise and keep trying until they find something that works. Most times, designers only know they are onto something when they see it. The life designer knows his life is well designed when he gets more than he put in.

"A well-designed life is a life that is generative— it is constantly creative, productive, changing, evolving, and there is always the possibility of surprise."

Design thinking can help you find a job you love, make a good living, strike a balance between work and family, and make a difference in the world.

Designers find answers to some of the most pressing problems by reframing their questions. Using the information they have about the problem, they restate their point of view and begin working on a prototype. They don't fixate on the problem they have to solve; they focus on the people who will be using the product. By starting with empathy, they are able to see the point of view of end users and craft products that meet their needs.

Life design starts with a similar reframe. Instead of asking what you want to be when you grow up, you ask yourself what you want to grow into because there is no perfect plan, no single solution. There are many possibilities and many designs, and each becomes manifest with every turn your life takes. There are many versions of you, and each of them is right. The goal of life design is to help you live to the full potential of the version you are currently living.

Before you begin life design, you have to adopt the mindset of a designer. Designers don't merely think their way to solutions; they build prototypes and try different possibilities. You can't redesign your life by thinking about the change you want; you have to go out and build your ideal future, prototype by prototype. The five mindsets that will help you with this process are curiosity, awareness, bias to action, reframing, and radical collaboration. You have to be curious to see possibilities, test things to see what really works, reframe dysfunctional beliefs to find the life you want, embrace the process to forget the destination, and find a supportive community to bring out your best ideas.

Designing the process is important because most people don't know what they are passionate about or what they want to grow into. For most people, passion comes after trying something, liking it, and developing mastery. Since most people are passionate about many things, the only way to find out what they really want to do is try out potential careers or lives and see what they truly love.

Key Takeaways

• There is no perfect answer to the life or career you want. Creating your ideal life is a design process that begins when you forget the destination and make the best of the current of the many versions of you.

• Anyone can use design thinking to create a meaningful and fulfilling life – a life that blends who you are, what you do, and what you believe.

CHAPTER 1: START WHERE YOU ARE

Design thinking can help you create a meaningful life regardless of your circumstances. The first step is to figure out where you are so that you can weed out the problems that are holding you back. In design thinking, problem finding and problem solving are equally important because there is no point in solving the wrong problem. People lose entire lifetimes working on the wrong family, money, career, or health problems. Those who are lucky fail quickly enough to start working on the right problems. Those who are unlucky but smart succeed, only to realize decades later that they shouldn't have taken the path they took.

A Beginner's Mind

Dave Evans, the co-author, went to Stanford to pursue a biology major partly because his childhood hero was a fictional marine biologist and partly because his high school biology teacher was his favorite. It took him two and half years to realize how much he hated biology and how poor he was at it. If he had a beginner's mind, he would not have assumed that he wanted to become a marine biologist. He would have been curious to find what marine biologists do. He would have volunteered at a sea vessel to find if the experience of sea life would really interest him. By closing his mind to one idea and refusing to let it go, he took two years to figure out what he should have known in two weeks.

A problem may seem like a significant problem, but as long as it is not real or right, solving it does not get you any closer to a life of meaning. Real problems are actionable. Any problem that is not actionable is a fact of life, a circumstance, a situation, or an inconvenience. Like gravity, you can't solve it—you can only work around it.

Gravity Problems

Most of the problems people struggle with are either unsolvable gravity problems or really difficult problems that require effort and sacrifice. Knowing the difference can save you years that you could lose working on the wrong problem. Gravity problems are either totally unactionable (like trying to get rid of gravity so you can move faster) or functionally unactionable (like trying to raise the average income of poets). When you accept that nothing can change gravity—and that trying to get more people interested in poetry is a really long shot—you are free to design other solutions to the problem of feeling tired all the time or struggling with a meager poet salary.

To design your life, you have to accept where you are and stop fighting reality. Statistics show that it is difficult to find gainful employment after being unemployed for more than five years. Most employers assume that a job seeker who has been out of the market this long is incompetent. Instead of trying to solve the gravity problem of changing the perceptions of potential employers, you can solve the actionable problem of appearing incompetent by taking volunteer roles and reducing the gaps in your résumé.

The Health, Work, Play, and Love Dashboard

To find where you are, use a scale of "Something is missing" to "I have enough" to assess how you are doing in the four core areas of your life: health, work, play, and love. Full health, which is the basis of a well-designed life, means you keep a healthy body and an engaged mind and actively partake in spiritual practice. Work is the contribution you make at your office, home, and community—not necessarily something you get paid for. Play is anything you do simply for the joy of it. Love has to flow from you and to you.

Create a table with a column for each of these areas and mark where you are: whether you are a quarter-way, half-way, three-quarter-way or fully settled on each area. Write a few sentences about each area and ask yourself if the areas that are out of balance are gravity problems. The health, work, play, and love dashboard gives you a quick answer to the question: "How is it going?"

Key Takeaways

• The first step to figuring out where you want to go is to find where you are. Assess your health, work, play, and love life to discover how you are doing.

• People lose entire lifetimes trying to solve the wrong problems. Nurture the curiosity of a beginner to objectively explore your problems and the range of solutions you have.

• Gravity problems—or problems to do with reality—are not real problems. They are not solvable because no one can bend, trick, or outsmart reality.

CHAPTER 2: BUILDING A COMPASS

Life design is a way to figure out who you are, why you are here, and why it matters. You found where you were by filling the health, work, play and love dashboard. The next step is to figure out where you want to go by building your life's compass. A reliable compass includes a definition of your Workview and Lifeview.

Workview is your idea of work: the reason you work, the essence of work, and what you believe makes up good work. Lifeview is your philosophy of the world and how it works; it is your idea of what makes life meaningful, worthwhile, and satisfying. Your Workview and Lifeview change with time. The point is not to have everything figured out for life but to create a compass for a life that is right for you for now.

The goal of life design is to create a life that harmoniously connects who you are, what you believe, and what you do. If your Lifeview gives you a burning desire to leave the planet a better place but your Workview has you working for a giant corporation that pollutes the environment, you will likely feel miserable because of the mismatch between what you believe and what you do. A good compass is your original creation, not a copy of someone else's. It aligns your values and ensures you don't sacrifice your integrity.

Workview and Lifeview Reflection

In about 250 words, write your view of work: what work is, what it means to you, what defines good work, how work fits into society, and what money, growth, experience and fulfillment have to do with it. Look beyond the work you do and try to focus on the reason you work. Take work to mean any service you offer others, either formally or informally.

For your Lifeview, write about 250 words of what matters most to you in life. Reflect on and write down why you are here, what you believe is the meaning and purpose of life, and how you think you fit into your family and community. Write your ideas of good and evil, the role of a higher power like God in your life, and the role of joy, peace, strife and justice.

After writing your Workview and Lifeview, try to find out where these views complement each other, where they clash, and what influence one has on the other. The more these views complement each other, the closer you are to living a coherent and meaningful life. Your Workview and Lifeview make up your compass; they are the tools you use to reorient yourself whenever you feel something in your life is not working.

Key Takeaways

• You don't have to have everything figured out or know where you are going. You only need to know you are going in the right direction.

• Your view of work and life are your compass for a well-designed life. You know you are close to your destination when you find coherence in your philosophy of work and life.

CHAPTER 3: WAYFINDING

A compass helps you figure out the general direction you should be heading to, even if the destination is not in sight. Since there is no single destination in life, no GPS to guide you, the best you can do to find your way is pay attention to the clues around you and use the tools you have. The first clues you have are engagement and energy. Paying attention to the way you do things and noting when you are or aren't engaged and energized helps you discover what is working in your life and what isn't, where you should be going and where you should stop.

Flow: Total Engagement

Flow is a state of being in which you are totally engaged in an activity because it's neither too easy to bore you nor too difficult to make you anxious. When you are in flow, you experience complete involvement because the activity you are performing matches your skills. Flow comes with a sense of clarity, calmness, and ecstasy, and time feels like it is standing still. In a sense, flow is a form of play for adults. A meaningful career is filled with this form of play.

Energy

Some physical and mental activities sustain your energy while others drain it. Tracking where your energy goes can help you maximize the contribution you make to your life and that of others.

It's About Joy

A Good Time Journal helps you keep tabs on the times you feel bored, restless or unhappy and the times you are at flow and having a good time at work. By discovering when your energy falls and rises and finding a way to do more of the stuff that keeps you excited, you can make your work a joyous experience without changing your circumstances. Following the joy, the excitement, and the things that keep you in flow keeps you on the right direction, no matter your destination.

Good Time Journal Exercise

Make daily activity logs in a paper journal and record where you feel engaged and energized. Specify as much as possible the work activities that keep you motivated. Every week or so, note down the trends, insights, and surprises you find. Keep the Good Time Journal for at least three weeks to ensure you capture all your work activities. Double down on the activities you enjoy doing and structure the engaging activities around the less engaging ones to keep your energy levels up.

Use the AEIOU method to guide you to make accurate and detailed observations for your journal.

Activities: What were you doing, what was the nature of the activity, and what was your role in it?

Environment: Where were you and how did your surroundings make you feel?

Interactions: Who or what were you interacting with?

Objects: What objects were you interacting with and what effect did they have on your engagement?

Users: Who was around and what did they do to make your experience positive or negative?

Go back in time and reflect on your peak experiences from past projects or assignments. Add these experiences to your Good Time Journal reflections as they offer invaluable insights into what keeps you engaged and energized. Reflecting on work-related experiences from your past is especially useful if you are in between jobs or taking on a new career role.

Key Takeaways

• Paying attention to the aspects of your work that keep you engaged and energized helps you find your way to what you should really be doing with your life.

• Wayfinding is about discovering the stuff that keeps you fully engaged and excited. Doing more of this stuff is the way to a well-designed life.

CHAPTER 4: GETTING UNSTUCK

Most people get stuck in careers that offer little personal meaning because they are too busy forcing their first ideas to work. Designers are good at solving problems because they know the first idea almost never works. By generating several ideas, they explore numerous possibilities and increase their chances of getting better solutions.

"You can't know what you want until you know what you might want, so you are going to have to generate a lot of ideas and possibilities."

Whichever area of your life you feel stuck in, the only way to get unstuck is to let go of your first, big, or perfect idea and generate lots of both sensible and crazy ideas. You must accept that there are multiple designs your life can take and all of them are equally great.

Designers like exploring crazy ideas because they know the biggest creativity killer is judgment. To generate all the possible ideas you need for your life, you must silence the critical voice in your head and allow yourself to make mistakes. The crazy ideas may not be what you end up with but they help generate other creative possibilities. You have to let your first idea go because the first idea is often the most obvious and the least likely to work. Your brain falls in love with your first idea because it wants to get rid of the problem you are solving as fast as possible.

Mind Mapping

Mind mapping helps you generate several ideas from a free and simple association of words. To begin the process, pick a topic of interest and write it on a sheet of paper. This topic could be an activity from your Good Time Journal that kept you engaged and energized. Circle the topic and, next to it, write down five or six things related to the activity. Go further and write at least three things related to each of these five or six items. Use any words that come to mind to complete this exercise. The words in your outer circle do not have to be related to the topic at the center. Limit the exercise to between three and five minutes so as to create free associations before your inner censor awakes.

After mapping your ideas, pick a few things from the outer circle that interest you and combine them to create a few concepts. These concepts can help you find the perfect circumstances in the area you feel stuck.

Stuck on Steroids: Anchor Problems

Anchor problems are stubborn problems that hold an individual or team down and forestall progress. They are better than gravity problems because they have solutions. However, anchor problems tend to feel like gravity problems because the people who struggle with them have been stuck on the solution that won't work for so long that the problem seems insurmountable.

When you jump to a solution too quickly, it's easy to lose your way, forget what you were really trying to solve, and anchor yourself to the wrong solution. Whenever you find yourself stuck on a problem, try to reframe the solution to include other possibilities and prototype these alternative solutions. Most of the time, people get stuck because they would rather stay where they are than admit the solution they have isn't working.

Key Takeaways

• There is no single best idea for your life; there are multiple lives you could live happily and different paths you can take – each as good as the other.

• Life designers choose better from a basket of several ideas. They never go with the first solution.

CHAPTER 5: DESIGN YOUR LIVES

A single right choice, no matter how significant, does not guarantee a good life because you will live different lives blended into one lifetime. There are endless versions of the life you can live. Knowing this opens you up to new possibilities and abates the pressure that builds up when the *perfect* plan stops working.

Embrace Your Multiple Personalities

The best way to design your life is to plan for multiple versions of it. You can create these alternatives or Odyssey plans even if you already have a preferred plan or are already executing another plan. When you start out with three parallel plans instead of one, you lessen the risk of prematurely committing to one plan and conceive even better ideas for your life. All the Odyssey plans you create are plan A—each is as important as the other because all are true versions of you.

The three alternative versions of your life you create have to be fundamentally different from each other. These versions are the possible ways you could live the next five years of your life. Life One is the life you have in mind or the life you are currently living. Life Two is what you would do if what you do in Life One were over. Life Three is what you would do if money or image were not a concern.

Write down the things you would want to test or explore in each of the three alternative lives. Include a visual timeline and a list of personal events that may accompany each alternative. For each version, ask yourself what life will look like if you implement it, what resources you will need, how much you like the plan, how confident you are about pulling it off, and how well it is aligned to your Workview and Lifeview.

Review your alternative lives—preferably in a supportive group—and note how each plan energizes you. These alternatives are not answers to the life you seek; they are possibilities that you explore and prototype to find what you must do next.

Key Takeaways

• The best way to design your life is to design multiple versions of your life.

• Creating three alternative versions of your career or personal life generates options, prevents you from committing to one plan prematurely, and guides you towards what comes next.

CHAPTER 6: PROTOTYPING

You can discover a future that interests you—a future you could not have thought of—by exploring the options you have through hands-on experience. Putting in hours of work, meeting new people, and using each experience as a launching pad to something better can lead you to an unimaginable future.

When it comes to life design, prototyping is not about creating design representations or testing solutions to see if they are right; it is about asking good questions, weeding out unconscious biases, and creating the momentum you need to set out on a course that appeals to you. Prototyping is a way to design experiences and give you a feel of what each alternative life might feel like.

The easiest way to prototype a life design is to have a conversation with someone doing what you want to do – someone with experience in one of your life versions. The conversation is intended to find out how the person got where he is, what his day to day life is like, and what he loves and hates about what he does. From this conversation, you can imagine how your life would be if you pursued this version of your life.

In addition to having prototype conversations, you can get some prototype experience by watching the person doing what you would like to do or by asking to do some of the work yourself. The prototype experience may involve following the person of interest around his workplace, taking part in a week-long project, or even taking up a three-month internship in your field of interest.

Brainstorming Prototype Experiences

Brainstorming prototypable ideas can help you create prototypes for your life design and help you understand what it is like to live each of the alternative life versions you created. To start off, frame the question you have about your alternative life into a brainstorming topic. Ideally, the brainstorming question should start with "How many ways can we think of to…" Gather a group of three to six people to come up with several unfiltered ideas that you can prototype in the real world.

After the brainstorming session, group the ideas you have collected into categories of most exciting ideas, ideas that won't work, ideas you wish you could pursue, and ideas that are likely to lead to the life you envision. Request your group to cast silent votes on the best ideas to help you decide which ideas to prototype first.

Key Takeaways

• Prototypes give you a preview of your future and help you fail fast and fail forward. They guard against the inclination to overinvest in ideas that would never have worked out.

• Brainstorming helps generate the ideas you need to create prototypes for exploring your alternative life versions.

CHAPTER 7: HOW NOT TO GET A JOB

The standard approach to job seeking where the applicant reviews job listings, finds a job that looks "perfect", sends a résumé, and waits for an invitation to interview works only about 5 percent of the time. This approach fails because applicants assume the perfect job is out there waiting for them.

Most job searches are frustrating because the first place job seekers look is hardly the place to find good jobs. Only about 20 percent of jobs are posted on the Internet. Most large companies post their jobs internally and only list them to external job seekers if word of mouth or social networks do not attract a large enough pool of candidates. The only way to tap into these jobs is to be an insider—to be part of the professional network of the companies posting these jobs.

If you still have to rely on the internet as your primary source of job postings, there are a few tips that may increase your chances of landing a great job.

Fit in before you stand out. Make sure your résumé ends up top of the résumé pile by describing yourself with the exact words the company uses. If you don't have the skills listed on the description, find a way to describe the skills you have with similar words. Most hiring managers conduct keyword searches on a database of résumés to ease their work. The keywords they use are often lifted from the job description. When you make it to the interview, talk only about the skills mentioned in the job description and focus on what you can do for the company. Stand out by talking about your depth of experience, but only after assuring the hiring manager that you have the skills the job requires.

Ignore job postings that have been open for more than four weeks. Companies looking for super-candidates to fill up a position end up burning out both the candidates and the interview team. Ask a person on the hiring team how many people they have interviewed. If the number is more than eight, the company either has unrealistic expectations or a broken hiring process.

Avoid phantom job descriptions. A company that has already selected an internal candidate will post a job description that matches the candidate's résumé, conduct some interviews as a formality, and hire the "best" candidate. If a company's job descriptions keep changing and its vacancies are quickly filled, its job postings are probably a façade.

Before applying for a job in a popular company, **use prototyping conversations to get connected to the people working in the company**. Popular companies can afford to let great candidates go. There is nothing you can do about it, but knowing someone from the inside helps.

Key Takeaways

• To maximize your chances of landing a job posted on the Internet, focus on the needs of the hiring manager, not your own, and present yourself as the ideal fit for the job in question.

CHAPTER 8: DESIGNING YOUR DREAM JOB

There are no dream jobs. What you find are interesting jobs with good co-workers. These are the jobs you can design to come close enough to a "dream job". Since most companies only post jobs internally (and it is almost impossible to be a job seeker and an insider at the same time), the only way to tap into the hidden job market is to become an inquirer—someone looking for the story, not the job.

While the objective of conducting Life Design Interviews is to help you find out whether a job of interest is something you would like to do, these interviews also give you access to opportunities hidden from most job seekers. The objective is not to get a job from the person you are interviewing, but you can ask how someone may become part of your interviewee's organization. By asking this open-ended question, you invite your interviewee to reveal opportunities beyond the current openings in his organization. Most of the time, the person you are interviewing realizes how interested you are and initiates an offer.

To get connections and referrals to the people you wish to interview, reach out to your contacts and have them introduce you to their contacts. Ask about the people you should be talking to about your interest. Most people like helping out and actually feel good about it – just as you feel good when you help out a lost stranger. Life design interviewing, or networking, is just a way of asking for directions to a community's insiders to get their stories.

Focus on Offers, Not Jobs

Most job seekers consider the nature of the job the most important factor when sifting through job postings. The problem is that there is no way to understand the nature of a job unless you work the job. You can't tell the ins and outs of a job from its generic description. And if you don't understand the nature of the job, you can only fake enthusiasm and pretend you will be a good fit.

When you pursue offers instead of jobs, you become curious about the nature and experience of the job and the people working in the organization. You become open to venturing out and evaluating all opportunities available to you, including the ones that you would dismiss as bad-fits. Your curiosity, which pushes you to have conversations with people about the nuances and best parts of their work, makes you an interesting person to the people hiring. In this way, curiosity increases your chances of landing offers.

Key Takeaways

• You don't find a dream job; you design it by exploring numerous opportunities, actively seeking out the people doing what you would love to do, and prototyping experiences.

• Networking is not a manipulation tactic; it is subtle way of asking for directions to meet the people sitting on all the hidden opportunities.

• Harness the power of the internet by reaching out to people whose stories you'd want to hear instead of sifting through generic job postings.

• Curiosity is at the heart of every design problem. Whether you are prototyping products, careers, conversations, or experiences, curiosity about all possibilities is key to landing the best opportunity.

CHAPTER 9: CHOOSING HAPPINESS

The ultimate goal of any life design is happiness. Contrary to popular belief, happiness is not a destination you get to by making the right choice; happiness is a process you master by making good choices and living into those choices with confidence.

The life design choosing process has four conscious steps: gathering and creating as many options as possible, picking the top alternatives from among these options, choosing the best alternative, and letting go of the other alternatives and moving on. When you start agonizing over your foregone choices, you postpone your happiness.

If you find it difficult to choose, the problem is not so much the quality of your research as your relationship with the options you have. Conducting more research does not help because it only reveals the things you don't know. Studies have shown that while the human brain is attracted to alternatives, it freezes when faced with more than five options.

If you have too many options on your list, cross some off so that you remain with (at most) five as your top alternatives. Don't worry about crossing off the wrong options—you will know when you do. If you still can't choose from among the five alternatives, either you are agonizing over the crossed-off options (in which case you should take a day or two off to get them from your mind) or the options you have are equally viable (which means you rest easy knowing any choice you make is a good one).

To choose the best alternative from the options you have, use more than one form of knowing to inform your decision making. Try combining cognitive knowing (the knowledge of the objective and organized information you have) with social knowing (the input of others), kinesthetic knowing (your bodily or gut responses), and spiritual, emotional, and intuitive knowing. To get better access to these forms of knowing, practice spiritual exercises, journaling, meditation, or yoga. These practices coerce the quiet and often shy forms of knowing to reveal insights to you.

Until you see the consequences of your decision, there is no way to tell if the decision you make is the best decision. Agonizing over foregone alternatives only undermines the satisfaction you get from your current choice and takes away from the energy you need to fully implement your decision. To be happy with the choice you make, you have to see your decision as irreversible, let go of the alternatives, and move on. Whenever you find yourself agonizing, remind yourself that the decision you made was the best you could have made given the choices and resources you had.

Key Takeaways

• Happiness is a process that involves making the most ideal choices and living those choices well. It is letting go of all of the alternatives that don't serve you.

• Too many options overwhelm your brain. When designing your life or career, cross off the options that are least congruent with your Workview and Lifeview.

• Whenever you are in doubt, *do* something.

CHAPTER 10: FAILURE IMMUNITY

Regardless of what you do, some form of failure is always going to find you. While no one can prevent plans from not working out, anyone can become immune to the negative feelings that accompany failure. When you understand who you are and design your life around this person, you free yourself from the fear of failure. Your prototypes may stall or fail, but every setback you encounter only gives you valuable information that you can use for the next prototype.

"Fortunately, if you're designing your life, you can't be a failure. You may experience some prototypes and engagements that don't attain their goals (that "fail"), but remember, those were designed so you could learn some things."

To develop failure immunity, you must nurture bias to action and try stuff out, prototype experiences so that you fail fast, and learn from your failures. By being quick to extract the value of failure, you lessen the tirade of negative emotions that accompany each setback.

Ultimately, life is not the finite game that you play to win; it is a process, an infinite game you play to find and become more of yourself. All of life's ups and downs are growth cycles, each giving you a peek into who you really are. When you adopt this mindset, every major failure you encounter is not an existential crisis; it is a reminder to do something differently, a redirection to the real you.

It helps to know that the sting of failure becomes less painful with each successive screw-up. It also helps to know that failing fast builds your immunity and lessens your inhibition to try out things that have slight chances of success.

Failure Reframe Exercise

To cultivate the failure immunity mindset, make a list of the failures you have encountered in the last week, month, or year. Categorize the failures into screw-ups, weaknesses, and growth opportunities. Screw-ups are simple mistakes you don't need to learn anything from—you merely need to acknowledge the mistake and move on. Weaknesses are familiar failings that you can improve on or accept as part of you. Growth opportunities are unexpected failings whose cause is known and whose solution is workable.

Zoom in on your growth opportunities and note what went wrong, what you could do different the next time, and what there is to learn. Build your failure immunity by regularly logging your failures and looking for opportunities for growth.

Key Takeaways

• Life design ensures you fail more often at the small learning experiences and make real progress in the areas that really matter.

• Failure is part of the long-term game of success, but only if you learn from it and use its lessons to make improvements in your life design.

• Failure, not success, is your greatest source of learning.

CHAPTER 11: BUILDING A TEAM

Radical collaboration is the magic process designers use to make genius creations. Like a good product design, a well-designed life is a communal undertaking. Whether you are finding your way, selecting among options, or prototyping, the contribution of others is invaluable because it is the raw material you need for your design. Your collaborators are your co-creators; they are the keepers of the wealth of knowledge you need to avoid tripping on your own myopia.

Everyone in your life design team has a role to play. Supporters are the people who encourage you on your journey and offer valuable feedback. Players are the people you engage with in your life design projects. Intimates are the people closest to you and the most affected by your life design—they are your family and close friends.

The members of your team are the people you share the details of your life design with. They don't have to be people you are close to; anyone willing to be there for you and to reflect and offer feedback on your design can do. Ideally, your team should have between three and five people with dynamic views.

Team Roles and Rules

The team is there to help you co-create your life design, not to offer financial or spiritual advice. The only role that needs to be clear is yours. As the facilitator, you schedule meetings and communication and organize the agenda. You ensure everyone takes part in the conversation and that key ideas are considered. The idea is to keep things simple and ensure meetings are confidential, respectful, and constructive.

It also helps to have a mentor—someone with a broad base of experience to offer you counsel, not advice. Unless you share the same values, priorities, and experiences, no expert can offer you the right advice for your life. Counsel helps you figure out your thoughts and insights. Good mentors mostly listen, ask lots of questions, and reframe the situation to give you a better perspective.

If you find the experience of having life design collaborators rewarding, you can look beyond your team and join a community. A good community is a group of people who share the same purpose and values, have the right intentions (not necessarily the right information), meet regularly, and focus more on each other rather than on the process.

Key Takeaways

• Every great product or building is the brainchild of a team of designers. Find a team of collaborators to help you discover your best life design ideas.

CONCLUSION: A WELL-DESIGNED LIFE

Life design is a process, a way of living. It takes time to balance your health, work, play, and love. Even then, perfect balance is unattainable. For this reason, the ultimate life design goal is not to live a perfect life but to have an evenly balanced life. A life designer aspires to live with meaning and purpose, to matter to the people closest to him, to leave a mark in the world, and to have fun while at it.

A good life design does not change you into a different person; it brings out the best in you and makes you more like you. It is about designing and living the life you want. For life design to work, you have to nurture curiosity, try things out, reframe your problems, understand that it's a process (so you don't give up just yet), and ask for help from others. These mindsets pull you out of any problem you are stuck on and help you discover the life you desire.

In addition to these five mindsets, you have to articulate your Workview and Lifeview so that you have a ready answer whenever you ask yourself how your life is going. Revisiting and recalibrating your compass every so often ensures you don't lose sight of what you are here to do. Additionally, incorporating practices—whether meditation, yoga, prayer, or reading—in your daily schedule helps develop your discernment and accelerate your personal growth.

Key Takeaways

• Life design is a continuous (and if done right, joyous) process that constantly moves you forward and only ends when you die.

• Life designers don't fight reality; they assess where they are, build life prototypes to find what works for them, live their choices with confidence, and move on to other versions of their lives when circumstances call for change.

END

SUMMARY
of
THE ONE THING

The Surprisingly Simple Truth Behind
Extraordinary Results

by Gary Keller and Jay Papasan

A FastReads Book Summary with
Key Takeaways & Analysis

EXECUTIVE SUMMARY

With more information than any other time in history, and with so many changes to keep up with, everyone seems to be rushing through competing priorities and accomplishing little. Deadlines are becoming harder to meet, productivity is on the decline, and work-related stress is at an all-time high. In this *New York Times* best seller, Gary Keller and Jay Papasan come to the rescue and offer a deceptively simple solution: do less to get more and better.

The ONE thing is a dominant theme in the lives of people who have achieved extraordinary success, from iconic business executives to decorated Olympians. The authors contend that success does not have to be a complex process guided by overthinking, overanalyzing, and sweating all the big stuff. All it has to be is a sequential process that begins with a deceptively small step: finding the ONE thing that makes everything else easier or unnecessary and doing it exceptionally well.

CHAPTER 1: THE ONE THING

In the 1991 American western comedy film *City Slickers*, Curly tells Mitch that the secret of life is finding and sticking to one thing. Mitch asks Curly what the one thing is, and Curly replies that it is up to him to figure it out.

The approach you take to whatever you do has a direct bearing on your success. Consistent and sustainable success comes from narrowing your focus to a few things that matter the most. When you vary your focus, your success varies as well. High performers achieve more than others—despite putting in the same hours—because they go as small as possible. They find the ONE thing that has the most bearing on their results, concentrate on it, and ignore everything else. They know that pursuing too many things spreads them thin and hardly ever gets anything done.

Key Takeaways

• To find your ONE thing, ask yourself what is the single task that, when completed, would make everything else easier or unnecessary.

CHAPTER 2: THE DOMINO EFFECT

When a domino falls, it transfers the small amount of potential energy it has to the next domino, and this energy adds up so that the fall that began as a simple "click" ends up becoming a loud "thud." A single domino can knock over another domino that is 50-percent larger. The implication of this geometric progression is astounding. If the first domino is two inches tall, the 23rd domino would be as tall as the Eifel Tower. That a small domino can topple—through a series of progressively larger dominoes—a domino as tall as the Eifel Tower may defy imagination, but it is a mathematical possibility.

In effect, this means that prioritizing and knocking down the most important thing, no matter how small it seems, can produce extraordinary results. Unfortunately, life neither lines up dominoes nor marks the lead domino for anyone. Finding the most important task is a struggle that successful people handle by lining up priorities anew every day. When you commit to tackling the most important thing before moving on to the next most important thing, your efforts add up and the little successes you achieve build up to the highest success possible.

Key Takeaways

• Achieving extraordinary success is a sequential process. It begins by identifying and tackling one right thing before moving on to the next right thing.

CHAPTER 3: SUCCESS LEAVES CLUES

Most of the companies that have achieved extraordinary success have concentrated their efforts on the single product or service responsible for their success. Intel has its focus on microprocessors, KFC on its secret chicken recipe, and Starbucks on its coffee. Sometimes the ONE thing is not the key source of revenue, but it is what makes revenue generation in other areas possible. Google's ONE thing is search, but it gets the bulk of its revenues from selling advertising. The ONE thing can also vary over time. Over the years, Apple has shifted its focus from Macs to iTunes to iPhones and, currently, to iPads.

The ONE thing is a success recipe for all areas of life. Most successful people have had one person—a mentor, caregiver, or benefactor—who contributed the most to their ascent. For Sam Walton, it was his father-in-law who helped him set up his first retail store. For the Beatles, it was their talented and industrious record producer George Martin.

The ONE thing is always there, lurking behind the success of any industry or sports icon. World-class performers have a single skill or passion that they have nurtured, with a singleness of purpose, for years on end. Passion invites consistent practice, practice develops the skill, and the skill—continually honed—makes the professional.

Key Takeaways

• If you don't know your ONE thing, your ONE thing is to find your ONE thing.

• A number of things could be important, but there is only one most important thing. Find it, and do it exceptionally well to realize extraordinary success.

PART 1: THE LIES
They Mislead and Derail Us

Myths and half-truths keep people from accepting the simple truth that success comes from focusing on one thing. For most people, buying into the wisdom of the ONE thing is difficult because mistruths have taken precedence and misguided their thinking and actions. Six lies keep people from maximizing their potential and realizing the success they envision: The misguided belief that everything matters equally, that multitasking can work, that success goes hand in hand with a disciplined life, that willpower is always on call, that life balance is attainable, and that big is bad.

CHAPTER 4: EVERYTHING MATTERS EQUALLY

It's easy for everything to feel important and equal, especially when there is so much urgency to get things done. But while equality works well in sports and social development, equality in any productive work is a myth. It is a trap that forestalls progress. Given that no two tasks are equal, getting busy knocking out a hundred trivial items from your to-do list is not the same as completing one meaningful task. Success is not a game of busyness; it is a game of priorities.

Although to-do lists have gained a reputation as indispensable time management tools, they are nothing but productivity traps. It is easy to feel obligated to attend to trivial stuff because it is on your to-do list. Adding items to a to-do list as they emerge and attending to these items in their order of entry is more of a daily survival tactic than a deliberate success strategy. Checking all items on a to-list does not get you any closer to success, just as solving the wrong problem exceptionally well does not get you any closer to the solution you need.

In contrast, a success list is short, specific, and built around success. High achievers know that only a handful of efforts are responsible for most of their success. It's a law of nature—just like gravity—first proposed by Vilfredo Pareto who noted that 20 percent of inputs are responsible for 80 percent of the output. A success list is built around this law; it leaves out what you *could* do (all the stuff demanding your attention) within the course of a day and redirects your attention to what you *should* do (the priorities responsible for success).

You can find your ONE thing by taking the Pareto principle to its extreme. Make a list of all the things you have to do and highlight 20 percent of the tasks that will be responsible for most of your success. Take out 20 percent of the 20 percent until you all you have left is a single item. This is your ONE thing.

Key Takeaways

• A few things always matter more than the rest. The thing that matters most out of these few is your ONE thing. Concentrating on it is your gateway to success.

• The most important thing to do is to do the most important thing and say 'no' to everything else.

CHAPTER 5: MULTITASKING

People who concentrate on executing one task at a time outperform multitaskers because the latter divide their attention between competing items and, consequently, do everything poorly. Multitaskers are easily drawn to trivialities. With the human brain having a change of thought every 14 seconds or so, it is easy for a person who's uncommitted to a single task to try to do everything that comes to mind at once. Other than the risk of losing sight of what's important, switching tasks exacts a time cost that is not immediately evident.

"The cost in terms of extra time from having to task switch depends on how complex or simple the tasks are. It can range from time increases of 25 percent or less for simple tasks to well over 100 percent or more for very complicated tasks."

Researchers estimate that people lose as much as a third of their working day reorienting to new tasks and bouncing back from where they left off old tasks.

It's easy to do two things at once, but it is almost impossible to simultaneously focus on two things. For both humans and computers, multitasking is a lie. Computers switch between tasks at such a high speed that users think they are multitasking. Even jugglers catch and throw items in quick succession to give the illusion of multitasking.

• Multitasking is a lie that wastes time, undermines quality, and damages relationships. The human brain cannot effectively focus on two or more items at once.

CHAPTER 6: A DISCIPLINED LIFE

The idea that successful people live a disciplined life is as common as it is unfounded. Success does not require any more discipline than you already have; it merely requires that you manage it a little better for success habits to kick in. You only need a little discipline, for example, to commit to doing things as soon as possible and develop bias for action. The people who appear disciplined are those who have developed consistent habits.

"You don't need to be a disciplined person to be successful. In fact, you can become successful with less discipline than you think, for one simple reason: success is about doing the right thing, not about doing everything right."

The only discipline you need to be successful is that of choosing the right habit and working on it long enough for it to work for you. Michael Phelps became the most decorated Olympian in history by committing to train seven days a week, 365 days a year, since he was 14. Swimming daily was the only habit he needed to earn this status. The ONE habit simplified his life because he knew exactly what he had to do. It also liberated him from the need to constantly monitor everything else he did.

Habits may be hard to form, but once they kick in (usually after 66 days, according to research) maintaining them is effortless. The investment you make in developing one right habit is well worth it because the habit makes all the hard stuff you have to do easier.

Key Takeaways

• Success does not come from taking a disciplined approach to everything; it comes from channeling energy into selected discipline that develops the one habit you need to be successful.

• Give your selected habit time to form before building on it or building another one.

CHAPTER 7: WILLPOWER IS ALWAYS ON WILL-CALL

The idea that willpower is at your beck and call, that you can invoke it anytime you want and use it to achieve the extraordinary, is a myth. For anyone who has tried, willpower seems to have a life of its own—it comes and goes as it wishes, sometimes when you need it the most. Still, it is undeniable that willpower—and in extension, the ability to delay gratification—is crucial for success. Willpower is a matter of timing. The way is not so much *where* there is will, but *when* there is will.

Like a cellphone battery, the amount of willpower you have within a day is limited and exhaustible. Use it to resist something tempting, to complete a task you don't enjoy, or to suppress an emotion or impulse and you lose a bar. When willpower runs out, you fall back to your default settings. If your default setting is an inclination to eat junk or slack, no matter how determined you are not to, that's what you will do. Most of the important work you have to do seems overly difficult because you have already used up the willpower you need to handle it. To make the most use of your willpower, do your ONE thing early in the day.

Key Takeaways

• Willpower, whilst being incredibly powerful, is an easily exhaustible mental muscle. Do what matters the most while it is still at its peak.

• Eat well to keep your blood glucose levels even and to extend the battery life of your willpower.

CHAPTER 8: A BALANCED LIFE

A balanced life is more of a myth than an attainable ideal. Dedicating time to one important thing takes time away from other things and makes balance impossible to achieve. Conversely, pursuing balance means you can't dedicate extraordinary time to your ONE thing. Extraordinary results require sacrifices and time negotiations because the magic of life does not happen in the middle; it happens at the extremes.

The myth of balance is especially damaging because balance does not make for a successful or well lived life; pursuing purpose and meaning and prioritizing what matters most does.

The dangers of living at the extremes are as real as those of living in the middle, and that's where counterbalance comes in. Counterbalance ensures that even as you pursue the extremes, you don't leave everything else undone. It mitigates the risk of going so far that there is nothing left to go back to. Counterbalancing requires that you separate your work and life into two distinct areas and be clear about your priorities. Prioritize your most important task at home and dedicate enough time to it so that you can go to work and complete your most important work there.

Key Takeaways

• Attending to everything to strike a work-life balance shortchanges everything—the result being poor delivery on both work and life.

• Ensure that all the areas of your life are active. Even as you dedicate disproportionate amounts of time to your ONE thing, don't go too long without counterbalancing. Let your responsibilities take precedence when they should.

CHAPTER 9: BIG IS BAD

Most people consider big results a bad thing because 'big' conjures images of something difficult, time-consuming, or intimidating. Most people would rather stay in the comfort zone of small than face the imagined implications of big: stress, loss of free time, and potential failure. What they don't realize is that thinking big opens them up to huge possibilities, to new things, and to extraordinary results. To think that big is bad is to put up a low ceiling on your limits when you've never stretched yourself to know what your limits are.

Thinking big informs big actions, and big actions are what make extraordinary success. Thinking big is not a preserve of the fearless; it is within reach for anyone willing to look past his doubts and learn. Study the habits, models, and relationships of people who have had a similarly big dream and learn as much as you can about them.

Nurturing a growth mindset invites you to learn more, overcome your perceived helplessness, and exert more positive efforts. When you entertain the idea that big is bad, your mind finds a way to work against big opportunities or outcomes. The only thing you have to fear is waste, mediocrity, and the possibility that you may not live to your full potential.

Key Takeaways

• Don't sabotage yourself by setting artificial limits on your potential. No one really knows their limit.

• Big thoughts, bold actions, and a willingness to fail create extraordinary success.

• Set vast goals for all the areas of your life and work towards them. Incremental thinking—setting small goals and constantly asking "what's next?" —is a slow and inefficient way to accomplish anything.

PART II: THE TRUTH
The Simple Path to Productivity

Success does not come from adopting the so-called success mindsets or mannerisms. No one became successful by dressing up, being punctual or working long hours. Most people succeed not *because* of their habits, but *in spite* of what they do. People waste entire lifetimes overanalyzing and overthinking their careers, businesses and lives when success down to something as simple as doing a few important things well.

CHAPTER 10: THE FOCUSING QUESTION

In a speech delivered to the students of Curry Commercial College, class of 1885, Andrew Carnegie—who was at the time the second-richest man in the world—opined that the prime condition for success is an exclusive concentration of thought, energy, and capital on the business that one is engaged in. He remarked that enterprises that fail are those that scatter their brains and their capital.

The focusing question is an unconventional approach to finding the ONE thing you have to concentrate on and, consequently, to creating and living an uncommon life. The way life works is that you create your own journey, draw up your own map, and devise your own compass. If the journey of a thousand miles begins with a single step, then a misstep will take you a thousand miles off course.

To ensure your first step is in the right direction, you only need to ask yourself one question: what is the ONE thing you could do that would make everything else easier or unnecessary? This question is everything you'll need to know where your life should be going and what step you should take now to get closer to your destination. It works remarkably well for anyone considering what to pursue, what skill to master, what legacy to leave, what contribution to make to the world around him, or how to develop better relationships. To answer this question is to find the first domino you have to topple.

Key Takeaways

• Life is a question: the quality of your questions determines the quality of your answers and, ultimately, the quality of your life.

• The focusing question—what's the ONE thing? —creates the roadmap for the big picture (where you should be going) and the small picture (what you should be doing now).

CHAPTER 11: THE SUCCESS HABIT

The habit of asking the focusing question is the most powerful success habit anyone can develop. This single habit helps you line up your priorities, get more done with less effort, and achieve extraordinary results. You can use the focusing question anytime you have to make a plan of action for any of the areas of your life—be it your physical health, spiritual life, finances, relationships, or your career. Enlist the support of your family or colleagues to help you practice the focusing question every day and make it a habit.

Key Takeaways

• Start each day by considering the ONE thing you have to do that would make everything else easier to unnecessary to clear your direction and make the most of your time.

• Make asking the focusing question a habit to achieve extraordinary success in the areas of your life you want to change.

• Stay on course by reminding yourself that everything else is a distraction as long as your ONE thing remains unfinished.

CHAPTER 12: THE PATH TO GREAT ANSWERS

The focusing question is a great question in that it is big and specific. Big and specific questions force you to think along these lines and, consequently, help you find great answers to what you are trying to figure out. For a business executive, a big and specific question would be: what is the ONE thing I can do to double my customer base in one year? This question is big and ambitious and has a specific, time-bound outcome. It challenges the business executive and forces him to look beyond standard solutions.

The answer you come up with to the focusing question could be a doable answer, a stretch, or a possibility. Doable answers are obvious solutions that don't require much thought or change. Stretches are within reach but require some research and an extension of abilities. Possibilities are the hardest answers to find. High achievers look beyond what it within their natural reach and operate on possibilities. They research and learn from the experiences of other high achievers who came before them, benchmark, and look for the next thing that builds off the work of their role models.

Key Takeaways

• The best questions—the ones that give all the great answers—are big (aimed at extraordinary results) and specific (target an objective within a stated timeline).

• High achievers think beyond obvious goals and stretch their abilities to find and live within the realm of possibilities.

PART III: EXTRAORDINARY RESULTS
Unlocking the Possibilities Within You

Implementing the ONE thing and achieving extraordinary results comes down to three things: purpose, priority, and productivity. Purpose is the big ONE thing you commit to, priority is the small ONE thing you focus on every day, and productivity is the action you take—informed by your priority and directed towards your purpose.

CHAPTER 13: LIVE WITH PURPOSE

Life is a series of decisions, and the quality of the choices you make determines the quality of your destiny. Your purpose informs your priorities, and your priorities determine the actions you take and the accomplishments you make. When your purpose changes, so does your life.

To string your daily actions into a life of purpose is to find fulfillment and happiness. Happiness has become an elusive concept because most people rebound between achieving and acquiring, never pausing to find meaning or enjoy what they already have. Without the knowledge of what matters to you, it is impossible to know how much enough is—be it money or ambition. To not know what enough is to live as a beggar.

Purpose brings clarity, clarity eases decision making, and expedited decisions inform the best choices and experiences. Purpose gives you the inspiration to continue going even when things are not working out. You can find your purpose by considering the ONE thing that would mean the most to you and that would make everything else easier or unnecessary.

Key Takeaways

• Happiness comes from structuring life around something bigger than yourself; something more meaningful than money or status.

CHAPTER 14: LIVE BY PRIORITY

Purpose gives you a clear picture of where you should be going. Priority guides you there. Without priority, purpose remains powerless. Your priority determines how you live each present moment, how you string your moments into powerful days and, consequently, how you achieve the results you envision.

To know the most important thing you have to do now, connect your someday goal to your five-year goal, to your one-year goal, to your monthly goal, to your weekly goal, and to your daily goal. Start by considering the ONE thing you have to do in the next five years to be on track to achieve your someday day. Ask yourself what you have to do in the next year to move closer to your five-year goal. Go down the time ladder to the point where you ask yourself what the ONE thing you need to do now to get closer to your daily goal is. Visualizing the process of attaining your goals enables you to think strategically about what you should be doing and expedites goal achievement.

Key Takeaways

• Your priority is the ONE thing you should be doing now to get closer to your daily goal so you can get closer to your weekly goal. Ditto for your monthly, yearly, and someday goal.

• Make a habit of visualizing and noting down the steps you need to take from now to get to where you want to be someday to increase your odds of success.

CHAPTER 15: LIVE FOR PRODUCTIVITY

You are always doing something. Even when you are doing nothing, you are breathing, thinking, and sitting or walking. The question is not so much *if* you are doing something but what it is you are doing. Achieving extraordinary results comes down to doing what matters most and getting the most out of the time you invest.

Productive people do more, record better results, and earn more because they channel the bulk of their time and efforts to the pursuit of their ONE thing. They devote stretches of time to their ONE thing, block out everything else, and protect the time they set. Time blocking is the most powerful tool for creating a productive day, week, month, or year. When you create blocks of time on your calendar for your ONE thing, you set an appointment with yourself. Everything and everyone else has to wait until you are done with your appointment. To increase your productivity, time block your planning time, the time you take off work (for vacations or long weekends), and the time you take to concentrate on your ONE thing. Set a time block of at least four hours every morning to work on your ONE thing.

The best way to protect your time block is to treat it like an appointment. Tell anyone who needs you during your time block that you have an appointment and you can't be double booked. If a superior asks you to do something during this time, agree to it but ask if you can do it at another specific time in the future. Most of the time, requesters don't want so much to have something done immediately as to know it will be done. To protect your time blocks from yourself and everything screaming for your attention, write whatever you think you need to do on a task list and get back to your time block.

Additionally, you can overcome distractions by putting up a "Do not disturb" sign during your time block or working in a secluded space. Ensure you have all the supplies you need beforehand and turn off your phone and e-mail notifications.

Key Takeaways

• If extraordinary results come from ONE thing, it makes sense to dedicate a disproportionate amount of time to your ONE thing.

• Align your vision with your daily tasks to achieve extraordinary results. If it doesn't help get you there, it's not important.

• Dedicate big chunks of time to your ONE thing and block everything else off to increase your productivity.

• Protect your time blocks to make the most of your working hours. Make a habit of reminding yourself that until you complete your ONE thing, everything else is a distraction.

CHAPTER 16: THE THREE COMMITMENTS

Anyone seeking to make the most of their time and achieve extraordinary results must commit to three things: mastery, pursuit of the best approach, and accountability. Mastery is a commitment to give the best you can to your most important work so as to become the best you can be. It is a journey, a continuous process of relearning and practicing what you already know and apprenticing what you don't.

It is not enough to give your ONE thing your best effort; you must commit to finding the best way to do what you do to get the most out of your time block.

"The path of mastering something is the combination of not only doing the best you can do at it, but also doing it the best it can be done."

When it comes to the pursuit of the ONE thing, you must take a purposeful approach and keep challenging the level of effort you think is acceptable. Whenever you find that you can't do better than you are already doing, find new models and systems that can push your achievement beyond the ceiling you've hit. Resist the urge to settle for what feels natural and comfortable.

The third commitment is to live the accountability cycle of results. It means taking complete responsibility over your outcomes. It means choosing to be the author, not the victim, of your life. Accountable people don't fear or fight reality; they seek it and acknowledge their role in it because they know this is the only way to find new, relevant solutions and achieve extraordinary results. To become more accountable, find an accountability partner—a mentor of peer who gives you honest feedback on your performance and regularly asks for reports of productive progress.

Key Takeaways

• To achieve extraordinary results, make a commitment to be your best, to find better ways of doing your ONE thing, and to hold yourself accountable over your outcomes.

• Find a coach to share your progress with and to keep you on track. Simply knowing that a friend or peer is waiting for your progress report can push you to get better results.

CHAPTER 17: THE FOUR THIEVES

There are four thieves that rob you of your productivity, the first of which is an inability to say "No." The way you handle interruptions, invitations, and pleas for help has a direct bearing on your productivity. The only way to protect what you choose to focus on—your ONE thing—is to say no to everything else. Whenever you say yes to something, consider what you are saying no to (because there's always a trade-off), or what task you are taking time away from. Make a habit of saying a plain no, or suggest another approach or someone else who might help if you can't bring yourself to say the plain no.

For most people, fear of chaos is what stands between them and extraordinary results. They can't bring themselves to accept that success is a messy process: focusing on ONE thing leaves other things undone, other people unattended to, and a lot of loose ends baying for blood. Giving in to the pressure may be relieving, but it erodes productivity. The pursuit of extraordinary results begins in earnest when you accept that anything you pursue with intensity invites chaos.

Poor health habits are productivity thieves because they limit your ability to focus and function. To sacrifice your health by staying up late, skipping exercise, or eating poorly in the hope that your outcomes will well be worth it is to make a horrible deal with yourself. Big energy—the substance that produces extraordinary results—comes from feeding your soul with meditation or other spiritual practices and feeding your body with nutritious food. It comes from making exercise a daily practice, spending time with your loved ones to raise your emotional energy, and planning your day around what matters most.

An environment that does not support your goals is as disruptive as poor health habits. You are bound to pick up the attitudes of the people you come in contact with throughout your workday. Make it your mission to surround yourself with people who support your goals and who are success-minded. Their achievements will influence yours. Your physical environment has as much influence on your productivity. Stay clear of distractions—be it T.V, e-mail, or chatty neighbors —to focus on your ONE thing.

Key Takeaways

• Make a habit of saying "no." Any request not aligned with your ONE thing can wait until your appointment with yourself is over.

• Embrace chaos as part of the process of achieving extraordinary results.

• Watch your energy killers. To sacrifice your physical, spiritual, or emotional energy is to sacrifice your productivity.

• Create your workspace in a supportive environment. Keep away from anyone or anything that does not support your goals to increase your productivity.

CHAPTER 18: THE JOURNEY

The journey to any destination, to any dream you imagine, begins with a single step. This step is the ONE thing. Pick an area of your life you want to grow—your finances, career, personal relationships, or health—and think how far you can go in five years. Now try to imagine bigger than that and work that dream backwards, going down the steps of what you need to do to the present moment. The journey to live the largest life possible begins by thinking big and going small. It starts when you narrow your focus to just the one important thing you need to do. Faith in your purpose sustains the journey.

Doing the best you can to pursue your purpose and live to your fullest potential is the way to a life of happiness, a life without regrets. In the end, it is what you didn't do, not what you did, that comes to haunt. Make every day matter. Align your purpose with your current priority and productively pursue your ONE thing.

"A life worth living might be measured in many ways, but the one way that stands above all others is living a life of no regrets."

Key Takeaways

• Success starts from the inside. To live an extraordinary life, dream the biggest you can, prioritize the ONE thing that will take you there, and have faith in your purpose.

PUTTING THE ONE THING TO WORK

Get the power of the ONE thing to work for you and bring clarity to your life by considering the most important thing you can do to make everything else easier or unnecessary. Consider the ONE thing you need to do to get closer to the goals you have set for each area of your life. Think big, and be specific.

Set time blocks to ensure you focus on your ONE thing, and make a habit of prioritizing the appointments you make with yourself.

Key Takeaways

• The pursuit of everything gets nothing done. Pursue your most important thing and everything else falls in place.

EDITORIAL REVIEW

Gary Keller and Jay Papasan dig through years of research to make a compelling case for a perspective that should be obvious, but isn't: you accomplish more when you channel a disproportionate amount of energy to a few things that matter the most. What makes this book a great read is the fact that anyone stretched thin, struggling to juggle work and personal life, or desperately trying not to give up on a dream that's taking too long – which is just about everyone – can relate to the myths and dysfunctional habits that that the authors dissect.

Anyone who wants to relinquish the feeling of being constantly overwhelmed and live a purposeful life will find this book an invaluable guide. The ONE thing is, in essence, the Pareto principle on steroids.

END

SUMMARY
of
THE OBSTACLE IS THE WAY

The Timeless Art of Turning Trials into Triumph

By Ryan Holiday

A FastReads Book Summary with
Key Takeaways & Analysis

EXECUTIVE SUMMARY

In *The Obstacle is the Way*, Ryan Holiday displays how an individual can use his obstacles to turn them into an advantage. It is an excellent read that can be used as a manual to develop strategies that help you overcome barriers no matter how hard they are. Ryan – thanks to his research and experience – shows how historical figures relied on Stoicism to not only conquer their hurdles but also use them to their advantage. Needless to say, this book shows how the obstacles standing in your way ultimately become the way.

INTRODUCTION

We face obstacles constantly in our lives, and most of us cower in terror as soon as we encounter something unexpected. We don't know what to do, and it takes a short while for us to become paralyzed with fear. But, what if these impregnable obstacles aren't so bad? What if we develop the ability to override them and use them to our advantage? What if we make ourselves so strong that we face them all without flinching? Well, it is indeed possible, and that's exactly what this book will show you.

Key Takeaways

• Obstacles paralyze you, but it's important to remind yourself that you can overcome even the harshest problems.

• Instead of doing nothing and letting the obstacles overwhelm us, we can turn these obstacles upside down and make them our biggest strength.

PART I: PERCEPTION

As we see and comprehend the events that occur around us, we develop our perceptions and decide what those events can mean. These perceptions can be our strength or weakness, depending on how we look at it, but if we become emotional, we only multiply our difficulties. To prevent this, we must master the ability to limit our passions that have so much control over us. Yes, it takes strict discipline and skill to overcome our fears and expectations, but at the end of the day, the truth will be crystal clear. This truth – neither bad nor good – will be our advantage to fight obstacles.

Key Takeaways

• Get rid of perceptions to unveil the truth and see things clearly.

• Turn your perceptions into an advantage by limiting your passions that control you.

THE DISCIPLINE OF PERCEPTION

Whether fair or unfair, obstacles are a part of our lives, and we encounter them at all times in our lives. These barriers themselves are not dangerous but what matters is how we see and react to them while maintaining our composure. Our reactions are crucial in determining whether we are successful or unsuccessful in overcoming our problems. Whether gripped by fear, desperation or a sense of powerlessness, it's vital to remember that we can choose not to give in to these feelings. Instead of running away from our complications, it's necessary to stop viewing them as problems in the first place. Once we choose to focus and see things for what they really are, we automatically gain an edge compared to others.

Key Takeaways

• It is imperative to control our emotions, maintain composure, and focus on our problems to overcome obstacles.

• It is possible to detect an opportunity in every disaster by perfecting discipline in your perception.

RECOGNIZE YOUR POWER

Rubin Carter, a heavyweight boxing champion, was wrongly accused of crimes he didn't commit. He was sentenced to prison, and walked out after 19 years, yet he didn't allow the outcome to affect him. Similarly, it's in our hands to break down or fight against the adversities we face, and this is the only thing we can control. Remember, situations aren't necessarily right or wrong, but it's our perception that makes us see things the way we want to see them. Regardless of what your mind tells you, and no matter what people want you to believe, the decision to view an event as a boon or a bane and convert these obstacles into your advantage lies only in your hands.

Key Takeaways

• There's no good or evil, but there are only our perceptions and the way we perceive things can make or break us.

• Recognize the power of perception that helps you identify advantages even in miserable situations.

STEADY YOUR NERVES

When we set out with high goals in life, risk and stress are almost guaranteed, but it's up to us to decide whether we're going to pull our socks up or back off when it becomes too much to handle. It's imperative not to get frightened and convince yourself to keep going as though you aren't affected. Because if you hold your nerves, you actually haven't let anything happen. Remember, your acceptance and defiance goes hand-in-hand here – no matter how desperate a situation seems, there's always a way through.

Key Takeaways

• When you encounter obstacles, steel yourself and shake off the negative stuff that threatens to bog you down.

• Nobody ever said that the going would be easy, so steady your nerves and be ready for challenges.

CONTROL YOUR EMOTIONS

Most people create problems for themselves by giving in to their emotions and panic at the first sight of trouble. Instead of coming up with a solution, many of us press the panic button because it's probably easier than focusing on the task at hand. This is the source for most of our problems, so the best way to confront obstacles is to keep our emotions in check. Develop the skill of freeing yourself from negative thoughts and focus all your energy on solving your problems. Emotions that don't change your issues are unhealthy and destructive. So, ask yourself if your worrying will change anything. If it does, great, but if it doesn't, you're only wasting time.

Key Takeaways

• Emotions can throw you off track, so learn to control them and face your difficulties without panicking.

• Use logic to defeat your emotions and discover the primary cause of your obstacles.

PRACTICE OBJECTIVITY

When you look at things, you have a perceptive and an objective eye. While the objective eye sees things as they are, the perceptive eye imagines insuperable complications, which means that the former tells you the truth but the latter imagines a lot more. Therefore, the objective eye is stronger, and you can face anything only when you remove yourself from the equation. For example, when you advise a friend, you are objective and give solutions because the problems are evident to you. Similarly, if you stop for a moment and pretend that the difficulties you're facing aren't happening to you, you'll see that it's easier to arrive at logical conclusions.

Key Takeaways

• Learn to remove yourself from the equation and practice objectivity to solve your problems quickly.

ALTER YOUR PERSPECTIVE

Our perspective comes with two components: a) Context – our perception which focuses on the larger picture instead of reality and b) Framing: our unique way of looking at things and drawing our own interpretations. There's a vast difference between the wrong and the right perspective, and this indeed is everything. With your right perspective, you can be sure that the right action is bound to follow.

Key Takeaways

• Remember that you can't alter the obstacles themselves, but by changing your perception, you can choose to overcome the obstacles.

• Do not allow irrational fear to conquer you, but instead, understand what it means and tackle it through the power of your right perception.

IS IT UP TO YOU?

When faced with obstacles, we have two choices: either complain and give up or face it head-on. These are our choices, and we must also be aware that some of these options will not even help us overcome our problems. Additionally, with perception, things are either in our control or not, and this is the fundamental difference that separates successful people from failures. We can focus on what's in our control and leave everything else that's not up to us. Even if there's a minuscule chance of succeeding in your endeavor, keep chasing it until it's absolutely out of your control.

Key Takeaways

• There are some things you control and a few others you cannot. Therefore, divert your attention to things that you can change because there's no point in complaining about things that you can't change.

• Never give up chasing your dreams until there's nothing you can do.

LIVE IN THE PRESENT MOMENT

During our lowest times, it's possible to feel like it's the worst time to do business or even to stay alive. But regardless of what we think, what matters is that the obstacles we face are in the present. The now. Stop thinking about what could have been or whether it's fair or unfair because you're only wasting your own precious time. Use your obstacles as opportunities to learn and focus all your energy on your present problem.

Key Takeaways

• Do not think about the 'why' or what a situation really 'means' because you're only whiling time away by spending your energy on irrelevant things.

• Embrace your present and stop worrying about the past since the past won't help you solve the problems that are weighing you down currently.

THINK DIFFERENTLY

Steve Jobs was famous for his ability to accomplish things. He believed that nothing was impossible and that one could create extraordinary things when aiming high. However, we are taught to be conservative or realistic, which ultimately becomes an enormous disadvantage when trying something new. Again, our perceptions play a significant role here. As our perceptions determine what's possible and what's not, they also determine the reality itself. When we focus more on the obstacle than the goal, the obstacles will be victorious inevitably. Therefore, it's imperative not to listen to everything you hear. It is okay to question and experiment, and although you might not be able to control reality, your perceptions will have a solid influence on them.

Key Takeaways

• Regardless of what people tell you, be open and question things when you believe that you can do better,

• Stop focusing on obstacles to such an extent that you forget your ultimate goal.

FINDING THE OPPORTUNITY

A study of athletes by sports psychologists reported that the injured athletes who felt isolated and depressed after their injuries later improved remarkably to understand their strengths and help others. They created opportunities using their own obstacles. Similarly, if you're suffering a severe loss or if your company fired you, stop panicking and use your time to experiment and find better solutions. Your struggle against your problems should polish you and prepare you to function even better than your previous performance.

Key Takeaways

• Use the power of perception to discover advantages even in the worst possible situations.

• See through your obstacles and snatch the positives to come out as a winner because no matter how alarming the adversity is, there's always a positive.

PREPARE TO ACT

Obstacles are rarely as big as we perceive them to be. You can either think that it's impossible to override an obstacle or prepare to act on it. Once you see things for what they are, you must act immediately. Armed with your right perception that's objective, calm, and rational, you'll be able to expose your obstacles easily.

Key Takeaways

• The worst that occurs is not really the event that threatens you. It's the event and the fact that you lose your calm and panic, thereby giving you two problems to deal with.

• See your obstacles for what they are and act upon them immediately.

PART II – ACTION

It's common to take actions, but do we take the right action? Not just any action is satisfactory. It's essential to take a directed action. It's not necessary to use force to take actions, but what's important is our courage. Slowly, with flexibility and persistence, our obstacles can be defeated. In other words, our actions are the solutions to our obstacles.

Key Takeaways

• When facing a problem, do not take the evasive route, but instead let your actions speak.

• Mere actions won't help; in fact, your actions must be deliberate and bold to dismantle terrible problems.

THE DISCIPLINE OF ACTION

As humans, we are built to take action. For instance, when you're about to fall, you automatically use your hands to break your fall, and you do it without a second thought. You just take action. However, when facing problems, we delay taking actions and ignore the real problem because it feels better to do so. Instead of pretending that the problems don't exist, it's better to face them with courage and take action. Embrace your obstacles with energy, persistence, and a strategic vision that helps you turn problems into advantages.

Key Takeaways

• Ignoring a problem won't give you solutions. Instead of turning a blind eye, face your problems and take action to find solutions.

• Embrace your obstacles with an energetic zeal and turn them into your biggest strength.

GET MOVING

Amelia Earhart – a woman who wanted to become a pilot – faced obstacles on her path simply because men dominated the industry. Later, she received an offensive proposition without any pay, but she took it up since she just wanted to start anyhow. That's how successful people do things. They just start, regardless of the circumstances they are in. Similarly, if you complain and whine while chasing your goals, your obstacles won't automatically budge because you haven't really done anything to get rid of them. Success goes hand-in-hand with momentum, but you'll have to create that yourself and get started right away

Key Takeaways

• Don't wait for the right circumstance because it might never come your way. Instead, take what you get and pursue it to be successful.

• If you want to be successful, you need to create momentum and take action instantly, rather than waiting for it to happen.

PRACTICE PERSISTENCE

When General Ulysses Grant tried to attack Vicksburg in Mississippi, speculations were rife that he wouldn't succeed, but he kept going. He faced many failures, and none of his methods seemed to work, but he proved others wrong when he emerged victoriously. If we want to conquer our obstacles, this is the message we must never forget: failures cannot stop us, and we must keep soldiering on until the obstruction vanishes. When you aim higher, you'll always meet people that doubt you, but you must practice persistence and never pay heed to the naysayers.

Key Takeaways

• Success isn't achieved only by pure genius. In fact, persistence – even when staring at failure in the face – is the key to success.

• It's understandable to feel discouraged when facing insurmountable obstacles, but it's never okay to quit.

ITERATE

Start-ups are rarely launched as full-fledged businesses. Instead, they prefer to launch products with only a few features. So, why do they do this? Well, they do this to gain feedback. Feedback often tells you where you're going wrong and where you stand compared to others. If you're struggling with your product and have faced numerous failures, then it's time for you to sit back and think about what your potential customers are trying to tell you.

Key Takeaways

• Don't be deaf to feedback. It's the fastest way to understand where you're going wrong.

• Grab opportunities to turn your failures into successes by keeping an open eye and understanding how the world works. Accept your failures because they ultimately help to show you the way.

FOLLOW THE PROCESS

When you've got something difficult on your hands, don't get weighed down by its difficulty. Instead, follow a systematic process of breaking it into smaller chunks. Once you finish one step, move on to the other and so on. This step-by-step process is a surefire way towards excellence because you're following a process instead of the prize. Additionally, while you're at it, it's important not to get distracted. So, chisel away and stop worrying about the results.

Key Takeaways

• You can handle obstacles when you manage them one at a time. Follow a process and focus on one obstacle instead of taking up everything at once.

• Do not allow disturbances to distract you from the task at hand. Excellence is nothing but following the right steps, right now.

DO YOUR JOB, DO IT RIGHT

Andrew Johnson – the 17th President of the United States – was a tailor before he achieved dizzying heights in politics. Even after he became famous, he used to speak about his humble beginnings with pride. Regardless of whether you're a tailor or a plumber or the CEO of an international company, work hard at whatever you do because you owe it yourself. It's not only your duty but also an obligation. Don't be so vain and full of yourself as to think that your work is beneath you. No matter what you're doing or where you come from, just remember to do your job.

Key Takeaways

• Successful people are never ashamed of their humble beginnings. Your job might be prestigious or onerous, but it's never beneath you.

• Remember that even if you're working at a place you dislike, you need to be proud of what you're doing and use it as an opportunity to learn and excel.

WHAT'S RIGHT IS WHAT WORKS

When Apple launched the world's first iPhone, it was far from perfect. Steve Jobs would have loved to include all the features, and although he was a relentless perfectionist, he knew that they had to compromise at some point or the other. Needless to say, the point is to get the job done, regardless of which way you choose. Instead of chasing perfection every time you set out to do something, you're going to be better off if you perform the best with whatever you have. Be aggressive and ambitious, but don't forget to be practical.

Key Takeaways

• Aim high, but focus on the process rather than perfection. Chasing perfection is good, but not at the cost of practicality.

• Make the most of what you have, and know when it's time to compromise.

IN PRAISE OF THE FLANK ATTACK

What do you do when you're stuck with what seems like an impossible obstacle? Do you barge right through the front door while forgetting that the windows and back door are wide open? Think about Grant who achieved victory by bypassing Vicksburg. When the odds stack against you, try to come up with a smarter approach and use your resources carefully. Don't think of your obstacles as disadvantages, but instead, treat them as gifts or assets that force you to become creative.

Key Takeaways

• Never treat your obstacles as your weaknesses. Try to find a way to convert them into your biggest strengths.

• Remember that your shortcomings only force you to become creative, even when you perceive them as weaknesses. Instead of becoming over-confident with your power, allow your obstacles to guide you.

USE OBSTACLES AGAINST THEMSELVES

Actions have many definitions. It's not always about roaring and charging-- you can also take a stand quietly and deliver results just the same. For instance, Mahatma Gandhi never fought against the British, but instead, he took the non-violent route and defeated them. Likewise, tackling obstacles doesn't mean that you attack them at all times; you can just withdraw and let them attack you, thereby using the actions of others to your advantage.

Key Takeaways

• Sometimes, an obstacle can be defeated by letting it attack you.

• Some obstacles are too tough to beat no matter how hard you try. With these barriers, you fall back and allow them to trounce themselves.

CHANNEL YOUR ENERGY

Athletes can tell you about the pressure they feel when they're on the field. Pressure can get to even the most seasoned athletes and send them packing. The famed tennis player Arthur Ashe felt the pressure too, but he channeled all his energy into his game and developed moves that seemed impossible to his opponents. Similarly, we find ourselves in situations that can weigh us down, but instead of succumbing to frustration, we need to use it to fuel our actions and become stronger than our adversaries.

Key Takeaways

• Do not fear obstacles that pressurize you. Instead, use those obstructions to push you and make you tougher and harder than your opponents.

• Be bold and loose physically, but exercise restraint mentally, thereby ensuring that you'll never snap under pressure.

SEIZE THE OFFENSIVE

Whether you're weak or brave, you'll encounter several harsh trials in your life that seem to appear exactly when you're vulnerable and unprepared to face them. While many people scramble in fear, others use the negativity to their advantage and become bolder. In such adversities, they come out stronger because that's when they are at their best. They use such events as catalysts to turn their life around.

Key Takeaways

• You will face many obstacles in your life, but you can win only when you use them as catalysts to spur you on.

• If you get past the negativity surrounding your life, you'll not only turn the obstacles upside down, but those very obstacles will also catapult you to success swiftly.

PREPARE FOR NONE OF IT TO WORK

Your perceptions and actions can carve the path for your success, but it's also possible that you'll face impossible obstacles no matter how right you are. You think and respond to all situations as best as you can, but yet you fail. You always look for opportunities and do everything possible in your power, but this obstacle doesn't budge. What do you do then? There are a few things you can't control, but you can always accept it with humility and keep trying because it's possible to turn even such unwinnable obstacles upside down. Be prepared for an event where nothing seems to work, and accept these obstacles and simply move on.

Key Takeaways

• Some obstacles are impossible to conquer, and no matter how hard you try, you seem to fail. When you face such impenetrable obstacles, accept them with humility and move on.

• Impossible obstacles aren't necessarily bad, and you can turn them around to your advantage by learning about them. Remember, these obstacles only help you hone your skills and become better with every passing day.

PART III – WILL

Your will is that incredible power that can stand tall and not get affected by others around you. Treat it like your trump card. When things are still in your control, you turn to action, but when they aren't, you unleash the power of your will. But, willpower needs to be honed and cultivated. Like everything else, it's an art that gets better only with practice.

Key Takeaways

• When things seem totally out of your control, you can always bank on your willpower to steady your nerves.

• Your willpower will never fail you even under the most ruthless circumstances, but you must cultivate it.

THE DISCIPLINE OF THE WILL

Perception and action aren't enough to overturn obstacles. The only training that comes to your rescue is your will. This crucial third discipline is always in your control because it's within you. It allows you to think clearly, calmly and efficiently even when there's chaos around. Needless to say, your will gives you the ultimate strength – the strength that helps you endure and derive meanings from unconquerable obstacles.

Key Takeaways

• Will is a combination of wisdom and courage that extends to all facets of your life.

• Other things might not be under your control, but your will is the discipline of your soul that resides within you.

BUILD YOUR INNER CITADEL

No matter what you think, nobody is born with innate abilities to confront obstacles. Likewise, nobody is born weak either. It's up to you to develop an inner citadel – your inner strength to challenge those barriers. Practice makes you perfect at anything you set out to do, and it's no different when you prepare yourself for hard times.

Key Takeaways

• Build your inner citadel that protects you from your adversaries even if they try to break you.

• Nobody is born with a strong or weak mind, but it's up to you to practice and nurture it.

ANTICIPATION (THINKING NEGATIVELY)

There are times when we feel that that the world is unfair. Nothing seems real or straightforward anymore. This happens to everyone, but if you're unprepared every time that happens to you, your path is going to be treacherous when you fail after trying umpteen times. The best way to get around this is to be prepared. Know that you can't control other things, but you can control yourself. Anticipate problems and be prepared, but when it's over, get back to work!

Key Takeaways

• Anticipate hardships when you set out to do greater things.

• The world is not a bed of roses, so prepare yourself well before disaster strikes.

THE ART OF ACQUIESCENCE

Great people like Thomas Jefferson, Helen Keller, and Edison were born with constraints, yet they knew that constraints weren't necessarily a bad thing. They found their strengths by using those very limitations. For instance, Jefferson wasn't good at public speaking, but he excelled at writing. Similarly, when life doesn't give you what you want, you acquiesce and go with the flow. Follow the events and see where they take you with the belief that you're strong enough to face anything.

Key Takeaways

• Constraints may change your direction, but they can't block or prevent you from arriving at your final destination.

• Always look at the bigger picture and go with the flow when you battle dangerous obstacles because you'll ultimately succeed because of your resilience.

LOVE EVERYTHING THAT HAPPENS: AMOR FATI

At the end of it all, after you've discarded your expectations and accepted your problems, face everything with an unfailing cheerfulness. Now that it has happened, what can you possibly achieve by crying about it? When you realize that you can't control something, love it and accept it because your endurance test will push you towards greater things.

Key Takeaways

• Complaining won't help when you face issues, but accepting them and loving them will propel you towards success.

• Disaster can hinder your progress, but it also forces you to start everything from scratch, thereby giving you the opportunity to come back roaring again.

PERSEVERANCE

Some people are persistent enough to chase a problem until they solve it. Persistence is good, but are you perseverant? Perseverance is not about one single obstacle, but it extends on to many such barriers until the finish line. We aren't fortunate enough to have one single problem in our lives; in fact, we'll have many. Persistence is about taking action, but perseverance is about willpower and they both go hand-in-hand with each other.

Key Takeaways

• If you pursue an obstacle until you break it, it is persistence, but when you prepare yourself for the long run and expect many such obstacles you're perseverant.

• Know that you'll get over every complication if you have the endurance to stick to it. Enhance your staying power and stick to solving a problem until it doesn't exist anymore.

SOMETHING BIGGER THAN YOURSELF

Some obstacles are bigger than us, and we feel powerless to do anything about it. In such situations, think about how you can solve it for others even if you aren't able to help yourself. Reflect on how you can derive something good out of it no matter how horrifying your obstacle seems. Instead of becoming hopeless, do your best to get out of it with a mission to help others. Once you do so, you'll see that your hopelessness reduce to a significant extent because you're now a man with a mission.

Key Takeaways

• You're just human, and you will experience obstacles that are bigger than you. In such a phase, embrace the problem and solve it for others to get something good out of it.

• When you stop thinking about yourself and try to help others, your strength increases while your powerlessness reduces because a purpose now drives you.

MEDITATE ON YOUR MORTALITY

Many of us – even with our flaws – think we are invincible. We forget our precarious relationship with life. We also forget that it could all be over in seconds if a disaster strikes. Incredibly – and it even sounds silly – many of us need to be reminded of our mortality. Death is not in anybody's control, but we can prepare for it and know that it will visit us all one day. It doesn't need to be a depressing thought necessarily, one can even make it an invigorating one.

Key Takeaways

• Death is the penultimate obstacle we will all face someday. It's not avoidable, but we can at least derive value from our mortality.

• Remind yourself that every day is a precious gift because you never know when it could all be over.

PREPARE TO START AGAIN

The law of nature is such that our obstacles will never end. Just when you kick one problem to the curb, another pops up out of nowhere, and this continues forever. But that's exactly what makes life worth living. Don't give up when you face many obstacles because it only means that you're strong enough to take on some more. With every attempt, you're only getting stronger and better.

Key Takeaways

• Our lives wouldn't be interesting if we never encountered obstacles no matter how much we deny it, so embrace those obstacles and come out stronger at the end of it.

• You will face one problem after another, but do not ever give up since you're only preparing for other problems.

END

If you enjoyed these summaries, please leave an honest review on Amazon.com...it'd mean a lot to us!

If you haven't already, we encourage you to purchase copies of the original books!

Made in United States
Orlando, FL
21 March 2022

15990826R00075